Introduction

E iti noa ana, na te aroha

This is being written by an upstairs window that frames calm sea and bush-covered hills. On a map of the Marlborough Sounds this view appears as Fish Bay, an insect bite between Kenepuru Head and Waitaria Bay, the kind of place a tourist might drive through without a shift of eye. Yet to our family it is turangawaewae, mother, healer, storehouse of memories, and for me, a place of inspiration for writing. It is here that I can deeply explore the well of energy that is common to us all; here that I connect with the greatest influence in my life, the voice of guidance that we do not want to name except to say that it is truth.

Fish Bay has wrapped itself around many people. In the days when the children's reading programmes were selling well, I recycled income by having a retreat house built, a place where people under stress could come free for one or two weeks to experience the gentle healing of the bay. I cannot tell the stories of those who came. They are not my stories to tell. I can only say that in the twenty years of its operation, we saw the little miracles of this place at work in everyone who stayed here.

Now our children are the guardians of the land, the houses and the family history. The ashes of my stepson Andrew Mason were scattered in the bay; and those of my father's brother, Uncle David, and his grandson Troy are under a large totara tree. Grandchildren have their placentas buried under trees now fully grown. Terry and I will have our ashes buried on the hillside in an unmarked grave, and for us it will be a final coming home.

In a sense, this memoir will also be a homecoming, About nine years ago, Penguin asked for an autobiography. I declined. They came back and suggested a memoir, which seemed possible because it was in a wider place, focusing on the gifts of life that make a person. It will be a collection of anecdotes, viewed from a place of deep gratitude; my only regret is that I cannot name every one of the people who have shaped my life in some way. I'm like a riverbed trying to identify all the stones that make it what it is. But to those who know me, whatever the context, I thank you, and want you to know that your goodness is part of my ongoing journey.

PENGUIN BOOKS

Navigation

a memoir

Joy Cowley

Navigation

a memoir

PENGUIN BOOKS

PENGUIN BOOKS
Published by the Penguin Group
Penguin Group (NZ), 67 Apollo Drive, Rosedale,
North Shore 0632, New Zealand (a division of Pearson New Zealand Ltd)
Penguin Group (USA) Inc., 375 Hudson Street,
New York, New York 10014, USA
Penguin Group (Canada), 90 Eglinton Avenue East, Suite 700, Toronto,
Ontario, M4P 2Y3, Canada (a division of Pearson Penguin Canada Inc.)
Penguin Books Ltd, 80 Strand, London, WC2R 0RL, England
Penguin Ireland, 25 St Stephen's Green,
Dublin 2, Ireland (a division of Penguin Books Ltd)
Penguin Group (Australia), 250 Camberwell Road, Camberwell,
Victoria 3124, Australia (a division of Pearson Australia Group Pty Ltd)
Penguin Books India Pvt Ltd, 11, Community Centre,
Panchsheel Park, New Delhi – 110 017, India
Penguin Books (South Africa) (Pty) Ltd, 24 Sturdee Avenue,
Rosebank, Johannesburg 2196, South Africa

Penguin Books Ltd, Registered Offices: 80 Strand, London, WC2R 0RL, England

First published by Penguin Group (NZ), 2010
1 3 5 7 9 10 8 6 4 2

Copyright © Joy Cowley, 2010

The right of Joy Cowley to be identified as the author of this work in terms of
section 96 of the Copyright Act 1994 is hereby asserted.

Designed by Anna Egan-Reid
Typeset by Pindar New Zealand
Printed in Australia by McPherson's Printing Group

ISBN 978 0 143205715

A catalogue record for this book is available
from the National Library of New Zealand.

www.penguin.co.nz

To my sisters Joan, Heather and Barbara, and my brother Peter, as apology for all the times I've forgotten to tell you how much I love you.

Contents

Acknowledgements

Throughout life, we have concentric circles of support, family, close friends who walk with us. I do not include my husband Terry in the list because he is one with me and I with him, but there are people who may not be mentioned in the book but who have had profound influence with their guidance, love, wisdom and laughter. These include my fellow trustees at Storylines, Francie and Terry Shagin, Michael and Claudia Scheffler, my cousins John Hanning and Jim Berkett, Ross and Judy Hardie, John Dew, Jillian Sullivan, Parehauraki Huirama, John Crowley, Mervyn Hancock, Carl Telford, Graeme Cowley, Anne Powell, Veronica Williams, Ng Seok Moi, Tracey Lewis, Triss Ranford, Marie Keir, Pat Coles, Robyn Belton, Shirley Young, Wendy Pye, Ron and Patti Gauch, Kent Brown, John Vickers, Maria Cowley, Janice Cowley, and the NY McCormicks.

The Sea Within

The sea is always there. Sometimes, in dreams, it rises up against the windows of my house, a great blue-green wall, shining, translucent, wordlessly familiar. I press against the glass, filled with longing, yet am unable to find the way out to it. Always in these dreams, the house is an alien thing, fractured by the density of furniture, each item named – corner of table, chair, stereo speakers, cup and plate, window frame – whereas the sea that sings outside knows no separation. It is all of a liquid oneness and it is the place of belonging.

The call is not so strong in waking hours. We all live with language that divides creation by possessing it with names. Words are the tools of my craft and years of practice have brought skill so that there is very little gap between the intention and the result on paper. Writers learn the shape and weight of words, how they react with each other, how to lace them together to give information not implicit in their literal meaning.

We manipulate language so that the mind works one way and the senses another. We can pare sentences into splinters so fine that they enter visceral organs without pain and the reader only detects their presence much later.

Yet now, increasingly, words answer the tidal call. Names of things press against the glass of the house, striving to reach the point where language disappears. Separation longs for oneness. I sit at the computer with words at my command, only to have them run wild in their own formation, so that they end up racing together like a flock of lemmings down a hill and into the sea.

My father, Peter Summers, could not live at a distance from the sea. He talked of his childhood in a tenement house in Wharf Road, Ayr, Scotland. He was the third of six children, the one who met the fishing boats, helping to unload the catch in return for a few herring or mackerel tucked inside his shirt for the family evening meal. He was a clever, lively child so attracted to the sea that his passion would have become his occupation had he been stronger, but the only time he lived on the sea was with his family on the voyage to New Zealand in 1926. Rheumatic fever left him delicate and all his later voyaging was done in books: Norse galleys, clipper ships, colliers, pirate boats, submarines, World War II destroyers – these were his vehicles, and he didn't mind which seafaring story we chose for him from the library. When his wrists and fingers were so inflamed they had to be strapped to boards to prevent movement, my sisters and I used to turn the pages for him. But as soon as he was well enough, he'd be down to the beach, fishing, collecting firewood, his mind filling up with dreams he could never fulfil.

His family came to New Zealand in error. My grandmother thought these islands were part of Australia and said she expected to see kangaroos hopping along the wharf. There was no money to move further than Auckland, much less to Australia, so my grandfather took pick and shovel work, helping build the Point Chevalier road, while my grandmother concerned herself with Peter, who had another bout of rheumatic fever. I have a sepia photo of Dad at sixteen in a hospital bed. It was thought he would not live the night, and my grandfather ran through the town to find a photographer who could record the boy's last living moments.

In fact, my father lived another forty years.

Eventually the migrant family moved to Levin, where my father, at twenty, met a beautiful seventeen-year-old girl, Cassia Gedge, whose mental state was as precarious as his physical health. They married, and moved into a cottage on a poultry farm in Roslyn Road where my father worked for a while. And in 1936, after a long labour, a daughter came feet-first into the world.

We begin life in the sea. Before birth, we swim like little fish in our personal ocean and we are not surprised to learn that the amniotic fluid surrounding babies has the same salt content as the sea. As children we have scooped tears on our tongue, licked a cut finger, and we have tasted crashing waves. This, like any other truth, does not come as surprise but recognition of a knowing already in us.

The sea continues to speak to me of a greater reality beyond the daily mental processing. It is metaphor for the awareness that is in every cell of the body, and it insists on the interconnectedness of everything. Always the sea whispers about the universe we would experience if we could escape from the limitations of our five senses; it tells us that beyond these senses, life and death are the same. For all of its dark depths, the sea represents light. I am drawn to that light and to that other metaphor, the one that takes my longing to the window of this bodily prison. The sea represents more love than I could ever hope to hold.

Fish Bay

It is early morning in the bay and an orange sky stains the sea with the beauty of shepherds' warning, while bellbirds chime back and forth like a thousand crystal bells. When we first came to the Marlborough Sounds, we were so astonished by this dawn choir that we could not listen passively but had to capture it on an old tape recorder, preserving it like bottled fruit to be enjoyed later in another environment. Now, we can listen in stillness. As the first notes drop through grey light, we sometimes shrug on homespun pullovers and sit out in the garden. Morning air is cool here, even in summer, and everything is so wet with dew it is as though the sea has crept up over the land in the night. The damp air smells of salt, clay, bush, mouldering leaves, grass seeds and honeysuckle, and through it comes a rain of sound so sweet that sometimes the only response can be a prickling of tears.

Early explorers wrote of the bellbird's song in their journals, and their accounts suggest that salty hearts melted, as did Keats' when he heard the nightingale sing.

Here is a description of a bellbird from Dr Anderson, the surgeon on Captain Cook's ship the *Resolution*, lying at anchor in Queen Charlotte Sound:

> . . . a small greenish bird which is almost the only musical one here, but is sufficient by itself to fill the woods with a melody that is not only sweet, but so varied, that one would imagine he was surrounded by a hundred different sorts of birds, when the little warbler is near.

If Keats had lived in New Zealand, how would he have written about the massed bellbird choir calling up the day? For that matter, what would Bach or Handel have made of it?

In this place, the dawn chorus is magnified by the configuration of the land. Fish Bay is small, about 700 metres across, and the steep bush-covered hill behind it forms a natural amphitheatre. For that half hour at dawn, the air shivers with electrifying sound, but to a lesser degree there is song here all day. Bird life is abundant – bellbirds, tui, pipits, robins, yellowheads, fern creepers, finches and sparrows. In autumn the waxeyes invade the garden and orchard, and I have reached for a ripe fig only to have a waxeye fly out of a fruit pecked to a hollow cage. As autumn moves into winter, the fantails follow us, picking up insects disturbed by our movements. Spring brings the courtship rituals, the cries of paradise ducks and weka nesting in secret places and the antics of tuis tumbling out of trees. On the beach, the oystercatchers, shags and grey herons work in pairs with much fluttering and squawking, while terns flutter over the water like scraps of paper, and gannets drop with folded wings on herring. We walk cautiously past the holes in the clay bank above the high-tide mark, for kingfishers are nesting there and they are paranoid about trespass. A kamikaze kingfisher exploding from a bank in a shrieking flash of blue and yellow demands respect.

In all seasons the bay is green. Three spring-fed streams tumble through dense shade to the lower slopes, where waters are slowed by mats of cress, marsh buttercup and flax roots before flowing out to the stony beach, making channels that shift with floods.

The land is now reclaiming its forest, after being cleared and then farmed for nearly eighty years. It was bought in 1885 by James McMahon, who built a small house on a high plateau at the western side of the bay. In 1971, when we tramped through the manuka and fern in the area, we found a small clearing and a fireplace with part of a chimney, built of red bricks made in Christchurch in 1886.

In November 1901, the farm was sold to Walter Mills from Hopai in Pelorus Sound. Walter married the daughter of a timber merchant, Elizabeth Ewing of Island Bay, and in 1904 a fine house was built as a wedding present from the bride's father, Robert Ewing. We were told that the flooring for the house was left over from a shipment of matai ordered for the House of Representatives. The rest of the house was of totara, heart rimu and kauri, with carved kauri framing four fireplaces, stained glass panels in the hall door, and a long front verandah overlooking the bay. The 'Showcase of the Sounds', people called it, and boats came in to admire the gardens that sloped down to the sea.

In the front room, between the fireplace and the sash windows that frame the bay, there is the original wrought-iron bridal bed in which people still go to sleep to the calls of weka and morepork and wake to hallelujah of bellbirds.

The farm was called Millig, although no one seems to know where the name originated. It could have some connection with the name Mills; but it is more likely a misspelling of Millaig, the coastal town in Scotland which has a similar land and sea formation.

Mr and Mrs Mills and their two children moved to Blenheim in 1916 and W P Henderson bought the farm. His son Austin lived there for many years and built a small cottage for his son Ron. Although three generations of Hendersons worked the land, it was never productive. Scrub claimed the steeper slopes, flocks dwindled, and the house aged without maintenance. 'Millig is hard yacker,' local people used to say. In 1963 Jim Ross of Lower Hutt bought the property as a hobby farm and holiday house – and that is how we first came to know Fish Bay.

Like many love affairs, it began on a moonlit night. My husband Malcolm Mason and I, my four children, Sharon, Edward, Judith and James, and their cousin Brent, were on Fred Orchard's boat *The Glenmore*, chugging across Kenepuru Sound at night, Easter Friday 1971. We had no idea of where we were going except that it was a long way from a Wellington suburb. We landed in darkness on a beach of wet stones, breathing air that smelled of salt and bush and sheep. Shrill birdcalls echoed back and forth and a brown feathered thing scuttled in front of our torches.

'Kiwis,' said the child who knew everything.

We found the old villa on the hill. It was in a poor state of repair, verandah fallen down, the moon shining through a large hole in the sitting-room roof, a pantry full of rubbish including empty baked-bean tins, beer bottles and a possum skeleton. It was basic, all right. A half-burnt pillow in the fireplace of one of the bedrooms suggested that someone had lit a fire before realising that the chimney was missing, and had hastened to stifle the flames. Yet for all its shabbiness, the house had a welcoming warmth and we quickly settled in. The children pushed up sash windows to admire moonlight on wind-ruffled water. But what were those noises? Possums? Wild pigs? Down came the

windows, shutting out all sound but the wind as it breathed in and out through the scrim-backed wallpaper. Hours later, when the children were asleep, Malcolm and I put on coats over pyjamas and walked the gravel road around the bay. The great round moon silvered the manuka and tree ferns and the lumps of sheep that watched us. We stopped at a point where the bay lay beneath our feet, moonlight across it like a ladder to the future, and I whispered in the awe of discovery, 'One day we will own this place.' Malcolm did not laugh. He too, had seen that quick glimpse of the future.

There was a tiny two-bedroom cottage on the property. We leased that for a couple of years, and then the entire farm went on the market, coinciding with the sale of the film rights to my first novel. The sums of money received and required fitted exactly, and our love affair with the bay became a deep commitment.

I could never say that I owned this piece of Marlborough; rather, it owned me, and it continues to shape me as a person and a writer. Stories of land and water have formed themselves as I've waded up the creek to clear the water supply after a storm, or sat in the dinghy fishing for the evening meal, or wandered along the beach gathering mussels: *Beyond the River, Sea of Peace, Cottage by the Sea, Tulevai and the Sea, The Silent One, Sea Daughter, Captain Felonius, Froghopper* and its sequel *Froghopper and the Paua Poachers.* Then there were the stories dictated by the brooding land and the animals that inhabited it: *Bow Down Shadrach, Gladly Here I Come, Shadrach Girl, The Tale of Tarama, Totara Hill.* In an orchard that celebrates freedom with wild apple trees, overgrown plums and pears, lemons, figs, quinces, I installed an imaginary well that would become a prison to the midwife Death in the story *The Well*. The old blind rooster who used to follow my voice, lean against my legs and coo affection, and who would attack visitors in a frenzy of feathers, went into his own story as *Rangi Tamahehe*.

Everywhere here there is story. I plant a windbreak of flax and, later, ask permission of the bushes to cut leaves to weave a peg basket. There's a story in that. Cold from winter fishing, I relax in a hot tub and think, 'Wishy-washy, wishy-washy'. Another story. An albino eagle ray follows my dinghy. A pet pig develops a taste for tobacco and eats visitors' cigarettes, packets and all. In a screaming nor'wester, a willy-wall picks up two kayaks from the beach and shoots them high in the air like missiles, dropping them in the bush halfway up the hill. On a calm day, I stand in shallow water and small fish, soft as feathers, lie on my bare feet to warm themselves. Stories, stories; and not just the inspiration, either, but also the energy needed to create them.

For me, Fish Bay holds the stuff of legend, and away from this place, I lose something of my identity.

The sun has now set in a dusting of yellow light that predicts a windy day tomorrow. In the tall kanuka outside this window, two bellbirds ring down the day with slow, separate notes. This is their bay. Honouring their ownership, I've put all the bush-covered land behind our dwellings in a QEII covenant in perpetuity, an idea that came from Keats' description of his nightingale: 'Thou wast not born for death immortal bird.'

For the bellbirds in Fish Bay, this is about as close to immortality as we can offer.

Story Beginnings

We are a storymaking species. As soon as two people begin conversation, story begins: reflection, opinion, observation. We document our past with story. We predict the future with story. Indeed, all societies are structured on and by story, history, herstory, and although much of this is believed to be true, it comes from human perception and therefore will always be incomplete.

So what then, is fiction? Is there any such thing?

I don't think so. What we call fiction is not so much creation as a rearrangement of experience, actual or vicarious. If I wanted to write a story set on the moon, I would research the experience of others who had been there, until their observations felt like my own; but if I were asked to write about something beyond all human perception, for example the description of a new colour in the spectrum, I would not be able to do it. Fiction depends on experience.

Obviously the historian or biographer has a duty to present the wholeness of factual material in a way that is interesting and informative. The non-fiction writer who is more concerned with filtering research through personal opinion, is indulging in subjective politics, and the resulting work needs to be considered as such. As I tell children who watch the television news: 'Remember that you are seeing and hearing what someone wants you to see and hear.'

Fiction also has its obligations. The first duty of the fiction writer is to entertain. The reader wants a well-paced story, told in interesting language, with strong plots and well-developed characters. In other words, the reader wants life – with all the boring bits cut out. The reader needs to be able to connect with the story on different levels. There is connection: *Yes, I've done this! I've been there.* There is empathy: *How could anyone else know exactly how I feel?* Then there is recognition: *That is a truth I've always had inside me but until now, I didn't know it was there.*

At the deepest level, fiction is a vehicle for the universal truth that is hidden in us all, truth that is rarely contained in factual writing.

When I was young, the only book that we owned was the Bible, but it seemed to us that every time we moved to another town, the new house filled up with story. Our mother was the keeper of the bible stories and, night after night, told us about Joseph with his coat of many colours, David who killed a giant with a little stone, Daniel who spent a night in a lion's den, Jonah who was swallowed – and vomited up again – by a whale. We particularly liked the 'vomit' bit, but we froze under the bedclothes as we were told about a stern God who saw everything we did and wrote it down in a book. Jesus was our hero. He was the children's friend. We decided to identify with Jesus, while God was dismissed like some grumpy old neighbour. But not all the stories were biblical. There were aunts and uncles who told us fairy stories and nursery rhymes, our Scottish grandmother who

told stories of her homeland, how she was a scullery maid in a big house and was dismissed because she ate some of the leftover food she had to carry in pails to the pigs. We loved that story, too. Then there were the cautionary tales designed to shape youthful character, written by people who forgot they were ever children themselves. *Boys, stop your noise! Girls, stop your dancing and skipping! And I will tell you about a rude, nasty, cheeky, dirty-faced boy who always deserved a whipping . . .*

I enjoyed the hero stories: of Grace Darling, who saved people from a shipwreck; and the Dutch boy who put his finger in the dyke and prevented a flood. Although I was only four, I had already learned that there are two authors to every story, the giver and the receiver. I could readily identify with young heroes; however, the vivid imagination I had inherited from my mother was tempered by a strong streak of my father's Scottish pragmatism, and I could not relate to plots that were weak on logic. Why was Miss Muffet scared of a little harmless spider? Little Red Riding Hood thought the Wolf in the bed was her Granny. I would know the difference between my grandmothers and a wolf. And why did Jack steal from the giant and then kill him just because he was a giant?

Even today, when I hit a logic hole in a book or film, I disconnect. Fiction must be credible. It must be true to its own reality.

I mentioned that oral story was connected to the different houses we inhabited. In effect, they were like books, each house a separate volume. I remember nothing about the cottage on the poultry farm where I was born; but there are mental pictures of the house my maternal grandparents had in Levin: a fish pond in the garden, and a polished table on which lay a fascinating object – Uncle Kelvin's guitar

– that I repeatedly twanged at the risk of smacked fingers. When I was three there was a little cottage in the bush in Whitemans Valley where I experienced a couple of unusual accidents. My mother told me to fetch my father, who was working on the other side of the garden. Instead of running around the path, I took a short cut across the garden, planting my bare feet in the hot ashes that had just been raked out of the fire. I stood rigid in the ashes, screaming. The next memory is of sitting in my sister Joan's cot, bars around me, my feet swathed in bandages. I felt very restless. I could see Dad sitting by the wood stove, reading the newspaper. I climbed over the cot bars and staggered to him. My bandaged feet slipped on the floor, I blundered against the hearth fender and fell forwards, placing outstretched hands on the top of the stove. Dad snatched me away and, through my crying, I saw the white prints of burnt skin on the black iron. I had been branded by fire on both hands and feet.

For a while, we lived at our Scottish grandmother's house in Ira Street, Miramar. Grandma and Grandad and three of their sons had a trucking business, and while the big lorries with their loads of coal and gravel crunched down the drive, my sister Joan and I played in the garden, having snail races which I always won because I trod on her snails.

Then there was a farm cottage in Ohariu Valley, near Makara, with a swamp in the backyard and wild blackberries in the front hedge; the house in Imperial Terrace, Kilbirnie from which I could see the 1940 Exhibition; the tiny concrete house further up the road where we lay in bed early morning, listening to the moaning sound of the foghorn and the clip-clop of the horse pulling the milk cart around Wellington streets. A great wobbly earthquake cracked that little house down the middle and we had to move to Johnsonville, where we stayed with Dad's brother until we shifted to a house in Bell Street, Otaki, that was flanked on two sides by the green sea of a market garden. In the middle of this garden, a man we knew as Uncle Joe lived in a tin hut with a dirt floor. He carved us spinning tops from poplar wood and told us about the wife he would bring out from China when the war was over. He also gave us little bags of rice and vegetables for our mother who was, I think, half in love with him. Mum was a very beautiful woman, greatly attracted to men, and I believe that her mental illness was exacerbated by the conflict between her passionate nature and her punitive religious views that denied its expression. As for Uncle Joe, I don't know if he ever got a wife from China. At the age of seven, I already had a sense that Chinese people were not treated well in New Zealand.

Those first nine years were governed by war, something we children did not fully understand. War was ration books, blackouts at night, rolls of barbed wire on Lyall Bay beach, and American soldiers who threw us candy bars and shouted 'Hubba, hubba, ding, ding!' at our mother. War came over the radio at breakfast time over the smell of burned toast – 'This is the BBC London calling' – and at school the boys drew pictures of planes like ducks laying eggs in flight. All of these were the normal furnishings of our lives; but there were dark threats that hung offshore, surrounding us with terrible fears we could not describe. Those fears had something to do with the faces of New Zealand soldiers in the centre of *The Free Lance* and the *Auckland Weekly News*, grainy grey pictures of the missing and the dead. Grown-ups cried when they recognised a face. The laughter at Grandma Summers' house was silenced when Dad's young brother David, a bomber pilot, came home with a shut-in stare and would not move out of his room. Shell shock, they called it. But for me, the worst thing came from my habit of listening to adults' conversations, my father talking over the tin fence to our next-door neighbour. 'If the Japanese come to New Zealand,' Dad said, 'I will shoot my wife and children and then myself.' It was only war talk, the kind that was stirred up by tales of rape and torture, but that my father should threaten to kill us all was a great weight within me that was not released until the day before my ninth birthday, 6 August 1945.

Four years ago, I went with Japanese friends to the Peace Memorial Museum at Hiroshima. Robyn Belton and I had an anti-war book, *The Duck in the Gun*, translated into Japanese and published by the Museum, and I spent most of a day there, visiting the human story of the atomic bomb dropped on Hiroshima. In that memorial to the cost of war, the pictures that still haunt me are the faces of children. I think now of the wisdom of a ten-year-old boy in a school in California, where I was doing a writing workshop. I had given the class a subject for an essay: 'What I would do if I was President for a year.' My young friend wrote, 'If I was President I'd make the people who wanted wars go and fight them.'

For a child, there is important story in every experience, and in preschool years, mine found its expression in obsessive drawing. For as long as I could remember, I made pictures on any clean surface: a wall, the endpapers of my father's library books, a smooth white pillowcase, with a piece of brick on a concrete yard or pavement. My efforts received more punishment than reward; but I remember a time when a young aunt poured praise over me: 'Look! She's done a lovely picture of Little Bo Peep and her sheep.'

I scowled. Couldn't she see it was me catching a rabbit in the rhubarb patch?

My sister Joan remembers me drawing on the tablecloth and then, after being caught and punished, crouching under the table to continue the picture on the rough wooden underside. I could not stop myself from drawing. While listening to someone, my hand would go out all by itself, take up a pencil, crayon, nail, any tool, and start making images. Always the pictures were about story. *This is the stove and the mother is cooking sausages for her children. This is a giant and he squashed the little chair.*

The worst punishment came with a series of pictures I scratched in paint with a hairpin on that part of the bedroom wall hidden by my bed. It never occurred to me that my mother might pull the bed out from the wall.

Today, when admiring the art of young children, I invite them to tell me the story of their drawing or painting. They usually do. Children make meaning of their lives through story, and storymaking begins long before they can read and write.

I came to reading later than most children, and for a number of reasons that are obvious in hindsight. We had moved around a lot; I wasn't prepared socially or psychologically for school; teachers in those days seemed to be employed by the punishing God who filled me with dread; and the phonics reading system had no meaning for a visual child. Like most children, I believed that when I started school I would read, and that didn't happen.

Some aspects of school were pleasing – new friends, drawing on a blackboard, playground games like skipping and hopscotch, making things with scissors and coloured paper or plasticine. But reading?

All I got was squiggles, black shapes on paper, white shapes on the blackboard. I had to guess what they meant and if I guessed wrong, a ruler rapped my hands or legs.

When I was seven, I was one of three children in the class who struggled with reading. We saw ourselves as being 'bad' at reading. We were failures. When we were kept in after school, the other two, both boys, went red and mumbled their mistakes. I cried. I had learned at home that, when punishment was imminent, the best strategy was to cry quickly and very loudly. It invariably shortened the whipping. But that didn't work with teachers as it did with my parents – and as well, I got taunts of sooky-bubba and cry-baby from other children.

Pleasurable learning leads to pleasurable recall. The reverse is also true. The significance of this came to me in the 1990s when a dramatised film was made of the childhood of three New Zealand writers. A young actress played a younger me, sitting at an old school desk and struggling with words, and the director wanted to make sure they had the correct reading book. They had an archival copy of the Whitcombe & Tombs Progressive Primer in front of them. Would it be all right if they faxed through a photocopied page so that I could verify it?

'Certainly,' I said. The confident, middle-aged woman stood in her office, waiting for a signal from the fax machine. A sheet of paper curled out and as I looked at it, my stomach knotted, my breath caught on the edge of fear.

It was an extraordinary reaction that had nothing to do with intellectual perception. It reminded me that childhood is not behind us but within us, and whether we know it or not, we act and react from it every day.

In those first school years, there must have been some accumulation of language skills. The breakthrough came when I was nearly nine, sitting in a standard one classroom in Otaki Primary School. We did not have a school library but there were regular visits from the National Library Service, a van full of books parked in the playground. Some of my fellow pupils were given thick books: *Treasure Island, Alice in Wonderland, Winnie-the-Pooh*. I had a picture book placed on my desk: *The Story of Ping by* Kurt Flack and Marjorie Weiss.

I don't remember struggling with words. I simply opened the book and entered a powerful story about a little duck that strayed away from home, got into terrible danger and came back home safe and sound. I was Ping lost on the Yangtze River, and I had that big frightening adventure in the security of my own desk and chair. I didn't want the tale to end, so I went back to the beginning and read the story again, finding that it was exactly the same with the second reading. I had discovered the constancy of print. For a child accustomed to oral story that varied with each telling, this was amazing. I lived in a world that seemed often unpredictable and unreliable, but here was something that didn't change. Once a story was put on paper, it was part of a something as solid and fixed as a mountain.

After Ping, it seemed that I instantly became an accomplished reader. I know that it couldn't have happened like that. I probably still struggled to some extent. The big change was in my attitude to reading. Reading was no longer a dull and difficult technical exercise that destroyed self-esteem. Reading accessed story and story was empowering.

When I was nine, my father took me by the hand to the Otaki Public Library, where stories were stored in box-shaped books that smelled of cloth, dust and glue. Dad knew the library well and had read almost every seafaring story in it. He talked to the librarian, who wrote my name on a card – Miss Joy Summers. Miss! She called me Miss! I stood taller, realising the importance of this interview. Yes, I would look after the books I borrowed. Yes, I would bring them back within two weeks.

As time went on, I was returning books in two days!

The children's section of the library was small and I soon ploughed through it, devouring Richmal Compton's 'Just William' books, R M Ballantyne's *Coral Island*, James Fenimore Cooper's *The Last of the Mohicans*. When the kindly librarian saw that I was not interested in British schoolgirl stories like *Monica's Last Term at St Cuthbert's*, she directed me to the big side of the library, pulling out the classics written by Dickens, Stevenson, Kingsley, Scott, Dumas, Hugo and so on. If some of the writing was beyond me, I did what most children do – jumped over those bits to chase the story. Sometimes, though, my ignorance tripped me up. One of Victor Hugo's books puzzled me because the main character, for whom the book was named, did not appear in the plot. I read the book twice looking for this man. No luck. The writer had forgotten to include the important character called Les Miserables.

After three years in Otaki we moved to Foxton, to another small town library and another kindly librarian – this one a grandmotherly woman who wore hand-knitted cardigans and had one eye. One pane of her glasses was as frosted as a bathroom window, and although I tried again and again to peer around it, I never managed to see the blindness behind the glass. But this librarian had 20/20 vision for important things, especially the heart of a child; and she, too, was a wise guide, taking me on a sure path through the big section of the library.

I learned from her that the people who said you only live once were not readers. As often as you open a book, you come to new places and live new lives.

I read every spare moment I had, but there were not nearly enough spare moments in the day. My parents were often sick, and as the oldest of five children – four girls and then, much later, a boy – I needed to work before and after school. So I stole time, reading a book as I walked to school, reading under my desk in class, reading during play and lunch breaks and again on the walk home. Sometimes, late at night, I took my father's torch to read under the bedcovers. Because I always put the torch back in the same place, he never found out. But he did write to the Eveready factory complaining about the short life of his batteries. He received a very nice letter in return, plus a box of new batteries, and I continued to read in my own place of light in the dark cave of my bedroom.

When I was twelve, a neighbour gave me an old bicycle. I didn't mind the rust and the loose chain. It was my first bike and now I could ride to school. Did that stop me reading? Not at all. An open book fitted neatly on the handlebars.

In those days there wasn't much traffic in Foxton, but even so, the dangerous habit had the inevitable result: I rode straight into the back of a parked van. The bike was badly crumpled and so was I, with two bleeding elbows, a grazed knee, a bump on my forehead, a broken nose and two black eyes.

If those injuries weren't lesson enough, there was more to follow. The next morning there was a special assembly at school. I had to stand between the principal and a traffic officer while all the students heard about the accident and what had caused it. Some of my classmates were excited because they thought I was going to prison, but they soon lost interest when they discovered I wasn't. As for the principal, Mr Morris, he said if he ever caught me reading on my bike again, I would be in very serious trouble.

He need not have worried. My parents could not afford to have the bike fixed and I had to go back to walking to school – reading a book.

At Foxton School we had a teacher who was fond of stern aphorisms like 'Empty vessels make most sound' and 'What goes into the mind comes out of the mind'. The latter saying certainly holds truth for children who love to read, for as they fill up with story, so will story overflow in their own writing. At an early age, the writing is usually derivative: children take the ideas and structures from the books they read and make them their own. It is right that they do so. We learn most things by a process involving four progressive steps: observation, imitation, innovation, creation. Sometimes teachers want to see brilliant, original written work from seven- and eight-year-old students who are at the second or third stage of development. This can happen, but usually children at this age do not have the background experience of life and language to be wholly creative. They build on the structures of stories that they know.

My early stories came from reading. Painting and drawing were no longer the preferred tools of my imagination: I had switched to words, spoken and written. From the age of nine until I left school at seventeen, I told my sisters Joan and Heather stories most nights. Our bedroom was our own place, a haven from the discord that often invaded the rest of the house, and on cold nights we'd get into the one bed, breathing warmth on each other as we became brave, adventurous characters who could overcome all evil. When a witch locked us in a castle, we unpicked the lock with a safety pin. When she raced after us, hurling thunderbolts, we jumped on the back of a dragon and flew away. There was nothing we couldn't do. Often we were on ships, either escaping from pirates or being pirates. We flew in imitation of Biggles. We swung through jungles with Tarzan.

These stories became more sophisticated as we got older, but always they followed the same format – long serials about powerful children who changed the world. My sisters now recall these serials, reminding me that at times I used to blackmail them. The heroine was left dangling over the crocodile's wide-open jaws, and would be dropped inside if Joan or Heather didn't take my turn at setting the table or washing the dishes the next day. Naturally, my memory is more selective and I would choose to be the altruistic heroine of my own storytelling. We laugh about this, and then soberly agree that in those stories, three relatively powerless children found a way to remake their lives.

An inkwell, a scratchy nibbed pen and an untidy child did not work well together. When the aphorism-loving teacher was added – the one who believed that 'Cleanliness is next to godliness' – then messiness became a grave offence punishable by the strap. Ink on the fingers. Ink blotches in the writing. Ink drawing scrawled in the margins. How did other children keep their writing books so neat and tidy?

'Joy Summers, please step out to the front!'

Once again, a hefty stroke of the leather on each palm – red stinging hands punished for untidiness.

These days I see, in the media, people of my vintage looking for compensation for cruelty they experienced in private institutions, including church schools. I am puzzled by the attention this receives. We were all, teachers and students alike, a product of our time. Schools were run to military standards. We marched into school in step, left right, left right. We placed our hands on the desks for fingernail inspection and were rebuked if our hair parting was not straight. My children find this hard to believe but people of my own age simply nod and laugh. It was the way things were.

I don't know what happened in private schools, but the upper primary classrooms in every state school I attended had the same kind of leather strap for delivering corporal punishment. I can only assume that it was standard issue. It was broad and thick, like the old-fashioned strop used to sharpen razors in barbers' shops. Teachers would wield it doubled or opened out; and either way, they usually swung it hard.

For untidiness! Often!

Well, at least one on each hand wasn't as bad as poor Ivan, who got six of the best – three on each hand – for giving cheek to the teacher. Six cuts made blisters stand up, white cushions against the red, so fat that Ivan couldn't close his hands. He showed us his palms after school. He was very proud of them.

In 1948, our standard five year, a boy brought a new invention to Foxton School – a ballpoint pen. It had its own ink and didn't need to be dipped or filled. We were amazed at the smoothness of the little ball tip, and how cleanly it wrote. We all wanted one. But Mr Morris announced that ballpoint pens would never be allowed in schools because they encouraged laziness and prevented a student from developing good handwriting. So we all sighed and went back to our scratchy nibs and inkwells. My stories and poems emerged, smeared and spattered, in exercise books that became dog-eared and torn by themselves. That had not changed; but something else was different – our teacher. His name was Mr Forsyth, he'd come back from the war to Teachers College and he was fresh in the classroom with new ideas that completely changed our attitude to school. This man saw children as people. He spoke to us as though our opinions mattered. The boys who usually sat blank-faced through social studies came alive to descriptions of cloud formations as seen by a World War II pilot, and were fascinated by accounts of ship-building on the Clyde. This teacher made lessons real and immediate and, best of all, he was full of story. We learned poems off by heart – Victorian ballads such as 'Lochinvar' and 'The Burial of Sir John Moore at Corunna'. For the last half hour of every school day, he read to us books: Stevenson's *Treasure Island* and H Rider Haggard's *King Solomon's Mines*. Behaviour in that room was exemplary. Any transgression was dealt with simply, without the strap: No story that afternoon. Oh, how good we all were!

What a wise man to use that time in the afternoon when children's energy is so low as to make them unteachable. He made a gift to us all of his great love of story. What was more, he didn't seem to notice that some of us came from struggling homes and were untidy, unwashed; he saw the talent beneath the messiness. He suggested that I send stories, drawings and poems to the Children's Page of the *Southern Cross* newspaper – which, of course, I did.

Through that teacher, I discovered I was a writer.

In the late 1970s I met Ian Forsyth in Palmerston North and was able to thank him for the difference he had made to his students in that class. I did wonder, at first, if he would remember me. His face lit with a huge smile and he said, 'You little pixie! You always had a book on your lap under the desk and you didn't think I knew.'

That was the kind of teacher he was.

I wonder if teachers know what a difference they make? Sometimes, in conferences, I have asked primary school teachers to reflect on their own school days and the subjects in which they excelled. Then I've suggested that success may not have been due to natural talent, but to the confidence inspired by the teacher who recognised it and fostered it. A good relationship with a teacher is vital for optimum learning.

If our standard five teacher helped us grow wings, these were neatly clipped in standard six by Mr Elder, who understood that although talent was a fine thing, it would dissipate without discipline. He was a man for detail, disliking sloppiness in speech, deportment, spelling and grammar; and I, eager to impress, tried to demonstrate newly found skills.

The school day began with morning talks. When it was my turn, I made a performance of it, preparing talks on 'The Rosetta Stone', 'The San Francisco Earthquake' and 'Louis Pasteur'. Other children were not so ambitious. One boy had prepared nothing and was told to tell the class what he had seen on the way to school. He started awkwardly. 'When I was coming to school, I seen the flax truck going to the mill. I seen some men . . .'

He was stopped by Mr Elder, who wrote on the blackboard: 'I SEEN'. 'Now what is wrong with that?' he asked us.

Up went my hand.

Mr Elder didn't see me. He looked hopefully around the room and asked the question again.

I shook my arm to gain his attention and, because no one else put their hand up, he had to come back to me.

'Please, sir,' I said. 'It's uncorrect grammar.'

He smiled and then started to laugh. He could not stop laughing.

As he turned back to the blackboard, his shoulders were shaking with mirth. He picked up the chalk duster, erased 'I SEEN' and wrote on the board 'UNCORRECT GRAMMAR'.

My face burned.

'What is wrong with that?' he asked, through the widest smile.

No one put a hand up.

High School

Midway through my third-form year at Foxton District High School, my brother Peter was born. There were now five of us, and, as always, lack of money was a problem. The pension never went far enough, and the need to supplement it was a responsibility taken on by me and my sister Joan. I don't remember any feelings of resentment at having to work when other children played. Actually, we felt a certain pride in being able to bring money home to help Mum and Dad. When I was ten, my Scottish grandmother taught me to crochet woollen headscarves in a lacy pattern called Solomon's Knot. These I sold in Mrs Hamer's bookshop for six shillings each, and I think people bought them out of sympathy. Foxton was a town that looked after its own.

Each summer, Joan and I collected lupin seed and sold it to the Catchment Board for one shilling and sixpence a pound. We also gathered mushrooms, blackberries and pine cones in season and sold them door to door. On a Saturday morning, we'd wheel our sister Barbara's pushchair to the local dump to gather scrap metal –

especially copper and·lead – and empty sacks, which seemed to be plentiful. These, our parents sold to a scrap merchant.

In the 1990s I told a large group of American teachers how poverty can encourage resilience and resourcefulness in families. I described how Joan and I sold things to earn money. 'At the weekend we went down to the rubbish dump, looking for sacks.'

There was an extraordinary reaction – an audible intake of breath, horrified faces, and a loud, 'Oh no!' I stopped talking, bewildered by the tension in the room. Then I realised that my Kiwi accent had been the cause of an unfortunate misunderstanding. I hastened to add that what we were looking for was discarded jute bags that could be recycled.

When I was thirteen and Joan was eleven, we found a job that was a regular source of income. We stubbed dead chickens at the Sandy Lodge Poultry Farm. Stubbing involved taking the pin-feathers and fluff off birds that had been killed, roughly plucked and hung in the cool room on racks. We got a penny a chook for this work and, although it was hard on our hands, especially in winter, we felt much satisfaction at being two of the best stubbers employed.

During high school years there were other jobs: house-cleaning, house-painting, shop work, waitressing. Each job brought new skills, new responsibilities; and the money at payday made life a little easier for us all.

There was a bonus that was all mine: I was never lacking new material for story.

I used to consider myself cursed with good health. My parents were ill, and my sisters took on every childhood ailment that passed through the town. Illness was interesting. It attracted attention in our household, and in the books I read. Elizabeth Barrett Browning, John Keats, Katherine Mansfield – would they have been famous writers without their maladies? The question bothered me.

'Strong as a horse,' my father would say, meaning it as a compliment. True, I could do the lifting, chopping, sawing that made him dizzy and out of breath; but as far as I was concerned that didn't count for much. While Joan, Heather and Barbara lay in their beds, covered from head to foot with measles, I was kept home from school as their nurse, to make them lemon drinks and sandwiches. I frequently lifted my singlet to see if spots were coming but there was nothing.

When we all got whooping cough, I felt encouraged. At last, I had an interesting disease! But while my sisters sounded like baying wolves, my little cough dried up before it became worthy of notice.

Physical strength did have some reward in that it made me Dad's fishing companion. He had an old truck and we'd go to Foxton Beach to set a longline at low tide. While waiting for the tide to come in, I'd use the bush-saw to cut up driftwood – a job I didn't particularly like – and we'd stack it on the back of the truck for the firewood pile at home. Sometimes Dad would light a fire on the beach, and we'd sit drinking tea from a thermos, eating Mum's scones, while he looked at the sea as though he was trying to talk to it with his eyes. On the full tide came the exquisite moment. I was allowed to pull the line in while Dad rolled up the legs of his trousers and waded into the surf to inspect the hooks. Almost always there were fish – kahawai, mackerel, shark, and maybe the prize catch, flapping blue and silver, causing Dad to jump about: 'Och, it's a bluidy big snapper!'

One Saturday morning we pulled in a snapper so big, Dad could barely lift it. Neither of us had seen such a monster. We hurried home to weigh it, but we didn't have scales, and neither did our neighbours. Dad refused to gut the fish because that would diminish its weight. The next day, the hunt for weighing scales extended along the street, but although people had cooking scales that measured up to two pounds, there was nothing to accommodate this magnificent gift from the sea. Dad had to wait until Monday morning. At nine o'clock sharp, he carried the snapper into Crotty's chemist shop and laid it on the big scales. Twenty-six pounds! Unbelievable! Mr Crotty admired it, but pointed out that the fish was quite bloated and might be going off.

He was right. Because the snapper hadn't been gutted, it had gone bad, and all we could do with it was bury it in the garden for compost.

Fiction is experience dismantled and reassembled in a new order. The stories I told my sisters at night had eclectic ingredients – scenes from Jules Verne, a gigantic fish, a team of children finding treasure in the skeleton of a wrecked ship on Waitarere Beach, the ghost of a pirate, a tidal wave. In the third form of Foxton District High School, the same fanciful adventures filled my English essay books.

The school was small: most of the students left when they were fifteen, and subjects were limited. There was no art class, which was deeply disappointing, but the young teacher who took us for English encouraged creative writing. She said she thought I had a future as a writer and that I should learn to type. Because she also taught the commercial course, she gave me access to the big Imperial typewriters after school, and supplied me with an apron for the keys and a book on touch typing. Did I learn to touch type? No, I was far too impatient. But I picked away at the keys and was soon sending my stories to the *Southern Cross* Children's Page, typed and in a more-or-less neat order.

Nineteen-fifty was not a good year at home, with my mother's sickness through pregnancy and after childbirth. We rejoiced in the arrival of our beautiful red-haired baby brother, but I was needed at home to look after him while Mum lay in bed, sinking into the mixture of delusion and depression that haunted her for much of her life. I missed a lot of school that year, and thought that when I was at school I was simply marking time like the rest of the students. Towards the end of the year, I learned that I could travel free on a bus to Palmerston North Girls' High School, if I took subjects that were not available at Foxton. I talked to my parents about it. They were not concerned one way or the other. I could do what I wanted as long as I arranged it and it didn't cost anything.

So, at the end of the year, I boarded a bus for Palmerston North, found Fitzherbert Avenue and Girls' High, and enrolled myself in a school that was going to be hugely significant in shaping my life.

Starting in the fourth form at Palmerston North Girls' High was a bewildering experience. My records from Foxton had earned me a place in the professional class, but I was far from competent in all subjects except English and art. I needed to take French and Latin so that I could travel free on the school bus, but this meant catching up on a third-form year in both. Every lunch hour there was a classroom reserved for detentions, with a teacher on duty, and it was in a corner of this room that I ate my sandwiches and pored over introductory languages. 'Translate the following into Latin. Where are the farmer's daughters going? They are going to the woods. Where are the sailors going? They are going to the woods. Where are the farmers going? They are going to the woods.' But in those days, the humour built into a Latin textbook was lost on me.

It never occurred to me to explain what I was doing to the girls in my fourth-form class. Later, one of them said they wondered what great crime I had committed, that I should be in the detention room every school day for the entire year.

At Girls' High I came under the influence of strong women teachers who encouraged initiative and independence. Katie Birnie, my Latin teacher, was very kind, a glorious mixture of intelligence and eccentricity. Elaine Worth gave me the run of the art room and talked as though I was an equal. Indeed, it would be true to say that I identified more with teachers than with my peers. The girls in my fourth-form class seemed so well groomed and sophisticated that they could have been another species. Sloppiness was still my trademark. If the hem of my gym tunic came down, it was fixed with a safety pin. A button would come off my blazer. So what? It still had one good button. The girls talked about things that didn't interest me: fashion, filmstars, make-up, boyfriends and dances. I wondered why they could be so interested in these things. They sensed my remoteness, and they acted as though I was not there.

In the 1990s I talked at a Girls' High reunion and afterwards was approached by one of my ex-classmates who was then herself a secondary school teacher. She said, 'We weren't very nice to you. We didn't understand you.'

I laughed and told her that I should be making that same apology to her.

The old Scottish work ethic was strong in my father's family. It was almost a sin to spend time and energy on anything that was not productive – which was why, I argued, sport was a waste of time. The truth was, I had been built for strength, not speed, and I was hopeless at all the popular sports, although I was happy to swim on my own or whack a tennis ball against a wall. Nothing in my nature or conditioning had, at that stage, led me to consider myself a team person.

When I was still at primary school, Uncle Kelvin, my mother's brother, taught me to box, defending with the left, jabbing with the right, and how to put a headlock on a person. Several times those skills saved me from playground bullying at primary school. I actually enjoyed fighting because I could win in a one-to-one scrap. I thought that if Girls' High had wrestling, I might have found a sport that interested me.

The old school bus left Foxton at 7.00 am and wound its way around the back roads of Oroua Downs, Glen Oroua, Bainesse, before settling to the main road into Palmerston North, arriving in the Square at 8.45 am. It reversed the route on the way home, getting to Foxton a little after 5.30 pm. This meant a long day; but because I didn't suffer from travel sickness, I had at least three hours of reading time.

There was the usual secondary school noise on the bus, a lot of boy/girl fluttering that made the journey seem like Pigeon Park in the spring, and at times I was aware that someone with hairy legs and short trousers was trying to attract my attention. But in that fourth-form year I was in love with the poet Keats, and no schoolboy could compete with that. In fact, it was not the kind of love that could be attached to anything ordinary. Keats himself had described the sensation that filled me when I read his poetry on the bus. 'My heart aches, and a drowsy numbness pains / My sense, as though of hemlock I had drunk'. Line after line, I drowned in his words, feeling them all addressed to me. 'Thou still unravished bride of quietness, / Thou foster-child of silence and slow time'.

The vast sense of melancholy was probably hormonal: I was late in maturing. But I would never have acknowledged anything so unworthy at the time. It was love. I knew it was love. My chest and arms ached with Keats' poetry. It made my heart flutter like a trapped bird in my throat. If only I could have met him!

When a homework assignment called for a biographical essay, I unleashed my love for John Keats in at least a dozen pages, and knew that the brilliance of the writing would move my teacher to tears.

All she wrote on the bottom of the essay was: *Keep to the facts.*

In my fifth-form year I would discover Milton and a wonderful contemporary poet, T S Eliot, but my relationship with them would be a little different. Even now, I cannot read Keats without hearing the noise of a crowded school bus and seeing the blank stares of sheep through the dust of country roads.

The fifth-form year was uneventful. I caught up with the extra school studies, worked Saturdays in the local fish and chip shop, taught Sunday school on Sundays, told the usual stories at night to my sisters Joan, Heather and Barbara.

Barbara, then six, was the most attentive, because Joan and Heather were drifting away to the adult world. They now had their own bedroom, their own secrets, and they read *True Confessions* and *True Romance* magazines. To tell the truth, I felt a bit lonely. Joan had always been my closest friend and now, it seemed, she and Heather had gone to a place where I could not follow. I spent more time with the little ones, Barbara and Peter, but my sense of belonging was shifting from the family home to school, and to the fifteen hours of reading time the bus gave me each week.

I did well enough in School Certificate exams and looked forward to returning to the sixth form, and to teachers who had become important mentors. But a perceived tragedy struck midway through the first term. For some reason unknown to me, my parents said I definitely had to leave school, go to work, and bring in a regular income. They had been considering this ever since I turned fifteen, but now they had made a firm decision. Perhaps they were in debt, or maybe they were worn down by the constant struggle. I didn't know. Dad told me I had to tell my teachers the next day that I was leaving at the end of the week.

Our sixth-form mistress seemed upset at the news. She sent me to Miss Wallace, the principal, who wrote down my parents' phone number.

I don't know what happened after that, only that one of my teachers drove to Foxton the next day to talk to Mum and Dad. Before the end of the week, Miss Wallace called me into her office again. The staff had arranged after-school work for me at the *Manawatu Daily Times*. The newspaper needed a new Children's Page Editor and I would be it. I'd no longer be coming to school by bus each day. I would live near the school with the Lloyd family and go home at weekends. The money I would earn would pay for my board and also assist my parents.

This change in fortune was so unexpected and so far removed from any image I had of myself, that I could not believe it. I'd had five years of writing for the *Southern Cross* Children's Page and thought I could manage the after-school job, but why would my teachers do this for me? I suppose I had not yet discovered the great human heart in the teaching profession that beats generously to a sympathetic cause. All I knew was that teachers had been parenting me since standard five, and this was the greatest example yet of their kindness.

Nineteen-fifty-three was a spectacular year that included Hillary's ascent of Everest, Queen Elizabeth's coronation and my change of name to NFC Lady. Yes, I was the News for Children Lady at the

Manawatu Daily Times. For twelve hours a week, after school, I worked in a small windowless office that I shared with the Women's Editor, writing on a big old Imperial typewriter that no one else wanted but that suited me well because it was the same as the one on which I'd learned to type. There was stained green linoleum on the floor, a bare yellow lightbulb above me and a desk marked with ink and scratches. It looked like a newspaper office. It smelled like a newspaper office. Everything in that room made me feel like a journalist.

In spite of the title, I don't think I ever put 'news' in the children's page. I changed the format to include children's writing, with publication earning points that could be accumulated to a total of fifty for a book prize. There were regular competitions, and every week the NFC Lady wrote an editorial, posing as a much-travelled woman whose spaniel Crackers got into awful trouble while she was away. Inspired by Archy the cockroach in Don Marquis' book *Archy and Mehitabel,* I allowed the fictitious Crackers to occasionally take over the typewriter while I was away, and the dog could then get its own back with an editorial about the bossy NFC Lady.

The staff of the paper gave me a free hand, and as long as I got the copy to the typesetting room by Thursday afternoon, I could run the page as I wished.

There was a tricky situation one afternoon, when a fourteen-year-old contributor in a Girls' High uniform walked into the office. She knew me by sight, didn't know why I was there, and was keen to meet the NFC Lady. 'Where is she?' she asked.

'Gone home,' I replied.

The girl said she would be back the next day and I hastened to explain that the NFC Lady had the flu and would be away for a while. The girl walked out, looking rather dissatisfied; but I thought I'd saved her from a greater disappointment. The nuisance of it was that I had to change the editorial letter to include coughs and sneezes, hot soup and boring bed with only a disobedient dog for company.

Weekday evenings I walked from the *Daily Times* to the home of Mr and Mrs Lloyd and their three children. Mr Lloyd was a Baptist minister, a kindly man, and his wife was warm and generous. Both took an active interest in their children, and were ready to include me in their family. Barbara Lloyd and I shared a room. She was a year younger than I and we became good friends.

At first it seemed strange living in a house where people didn't shout at each other. I kept waiting for something to happen. But gradually I became accustomed to the peace-filled rhythm of their days, and enjoyed it so much that weekends in Foxton became the time away from normal living. However, I knew that this idyllic existence was not permanent. At the end of the year I would definitely have to leave school.

Like many of their generation, my parents had not got past primary school. For them, education meant being able to read and write, and anything extra was superfluous. They were genuinely concerned that too much education was bad for children, especially for girls.

Near the end of 1953, the editor of the *Manawatu Daily Times* offered me a cadetship. Oh bliss! I had never heard of a girl being a cadet, and I could not wait to tell Mum and Dad. I would live in Palmerston North, interview people, write articles. Maybe I could stay on with Mr and Mrs Lloyd.

My news fell on deaf ears. Neither of my parents would consider me living away from home and working full-time for a newspaper. Dad was certain that all journalists were atheists and communists and said that I had already spent too much time under their influence. I would come back home and work in Foxton. Stuart Donnelly the chemist needed an apprentice. That would be a good job for a girl with University Entrance.

Pharmacy! I had not done chemistry or maths at school! A pharmacy apprentice worked during the day and studied by correspondence in spare time, for four years, to qualify. How on earth would I do that?

My parents made the arrangements – and in those days, we did what we were told. When school finished, I was to work at the pharmacy until Christmas, when I would go to Auckland to help my mother's sister Chris look after her three young boys. After that, I would come back to Foxton to begin my apprenticeship.

I said goodbye to the Lloyd family. They did their best to cheer me. They too were going to Auckland for the summer holidays, all of them except Barbara who, like me, would be working in a shop until Christmas Eve. We decided that she and I would go on the train together from Palmerston North.

The last day at school was pain-ridden. My sixth-form classmates were all returning to the seventh form. I was saying farewell to a time and place that was dear to me, and the separation felt like amputation. I wanted to say something to the teachers who had been my friends and mentors; but they were busy talking to parents. The atmosphere of celebration and laughter did not help the grief I felt as I walked towards the gate, my suitcase heavy with books.

I was outside the gate when I heard someone call my name. It was my English teacher, Rosemary Callendar, who was running down the drive. She had a favour to ask. Please, could she have the exercise book filled with my writing?

Oh yes, a thousand times yes! I was so eager to unclip my case, that books spread themselves over the driveway. I snatched up my writing book and gave it to her. She held it against herself as though she thought it of value. 'Please,' she said, 'promise me that you will never give up writing.'

Just as eagerly, I promised.

I never saw her again, and at that time, neither of us could have known how important that promise was.

I started work in the pharmacy and, in spite of my fears, enjoyed it from the first day. It was shop work. I had the Christmas holidays before I began the apprenticeship and serious study. I was also looking forward to the bus trip to Palmerston North station where I would meet Barbara Lloyd and travel with her by train to Auckland.

My pre-Christmas introduction to the chemist shop was not as long as planned. In Takapuna, my Aunty Chris became ill and needed me to help with the boys. I had to change my reservation and go to Auckland on 16 December.

On Christmas Day Aunty Chris turned on the radio and we learned that a train had been swept away at Tangiwai.

Barbara's body was never found.

Pharmacy Years

Here in the bay, land and sea teach us all we need to know to live in this place. The wild nettles lose their sting in a delicious soup, and you can make a different soup for the garden by soaking nettles in a bucket of water for a couple of weeks. Dilute the solution and water vegetables with it, for giant crops. Salads are gathered from watercress, fennel, the native celery growing near the beach and the tender new fronds of ferns. If you need a soporific stronger than the sounds of wind and sea, the inner bark of the manuka makes drowsy tea, and kawakawa leaves are always good to poultice skin infections. The gel at the base of the flax stalk is a laxative but to be used in moderation. A pot of boiling gum leaves clears a head cold.

It seems right, in this place, to gather the gifts of the earth for health, since this was the basis of my pharmacy training. In the early 1950s drugs were not synthesised and antibiotics were very new, limited in the dispensary to penicillin lozenges and tablets, and aureomycin ointment. Most medicine was made from natural products. Digitalis tablets for the heart came from dried foxglove leaves; and rhubarb, peppermint and baking soda were mixed to soothe indigestion. We did quantitative and qualitative analysis to determine the strength of plant stuff such as licorice bark, quassia chips and dried rosehips, because the potency of nature could vary with place and season. We disguised the bitter taste of plant alkaloid with thick sugar syrup that I boiled in the kitchen at the back of the dispensary.

While still at high school, I read the Greek definitions of four kinds of love: *eros* or romantic love; *agape*, kindly love; *philia*, friendly love; and *storge*, love for family. But I always thought that an important love had been omitted: a love of learning. The space for it is obvious in the curiosity of the young child. Satisfying that love is like drinking salt water, in that it increases the thirst for knowledge.

What pleasure there is in stepping over the threshold of the familiar to something new! So many doors to be opened! It seemed that every time the earth turned, it brought the gifts of new discoveries.

Far from being a time of trial and disappointment, the pharmacy apprenticeship in Foxton's only chemist shop was an exciting adventure. The solitary, introspective girl found a place in the township. The simple act of serving customers meant movement from acquaintance, to friendship, to strong family feeling, as local people interacted with me and told me their stories. In the dispensary, I mixed ointments for eczema on a glass slab; measured the ingredients for vitamin tonics – riboflavine, syr ferri phos, syr glycerophos, syr ribena, pulv tragacanth – and went home with purple hands after making gentian violet capsules for threadworms. True, the correspondence papers that arrived from the Pharmacy College in Wellington were daunting, and I needed help with organic and inorganic chemistry, but my boss Stuart Donnelly was supportive, as were the shop girls who taught me about Max Factor and Paul Duval make-up and which films fitted which cameras.

Every day, it seemed, I learned something new, and while that in itself was immensely gratifying, the greatest pleasure came from a feeling that I was contributing to a community who saw me as one of their own.

Some of that celebration went into a biographical story that I wrote about thirty years ago. Names of most of the characters have been changed, some dialogue reconstructed; otherwise, the story is true, and I resurrect it here because it best describes the pharmacy years – and a fervent desire I had to own a motorbike.

The year was 1954. I was seventeen and certain of my maturity. In the backyard of our family home at 32 Union Street, Foxton, my father was at his sawbench cutting wood. The blade screamed through logs, changing pitch against nails and pockets of sand; but Dad was deaf and heard none of it. When I tapped him on the shoulder, he switched off the saw. I wrote on a scrap of paper, *Can I have a motorbike?*

'What'll ye do for money?' he asked.

I scribbled. *I'll save.*

One side of his face lifted in a laconic smile. 'Aye, the blazes ye will. Too many bluidy books.'

The truth of it made me angry. I was in the first year of a pharmacy apprenticeship, earning three pounds, five shillings a week. Two pounds went to my parents, a small amount on Pharmacy College fees and the rest disappeared in the local bookshop. I underlined the last two words on the paper, then added, *I'll work at nights and weekends.* In large letters, I wrote, *PLEASE.*

Dad grinned. 'We'll see how ye mend yer spendthrift ways.'

My mother was entertaining in the kitchen. She asked, 'What did he say?'

'I'm allowed to,' I answered.

Her friend from the church guild gave an anxious laugh. 'Young ladies don't ride motorbikes.'

'I do,' I told her.

'She's got her licence,' said my mother. 'We reckon she should have been a boy. She can use a hammer and saw as good as her father, lay concrete, do soldering –'

I went into my bedroom, fell on the bed and listened to her voice coming through the wall. I'd heard the words so often, my mouth could shape them.

'– It was never any good putting her in a decent dress. She'd rip it getting over the nearest barbed-wire fence or wrestling with the rough children at school. You could never keep her tidy. If I dressed her in sugar sacks, she wouldn't have cared.'

But she did care. She cared, she cared.

Throughout childhood I had a deep yearning for beautiful clothes, for ribbons and laces and dresses with ruffles. Why was it not possible to have this as well as bows and arrows?

The mirror showed a solid girl with a plain round face and turned-up nose, but that was only the external view. Underneath, she was slender, graceful and devastatingly beautiful. She wore an Edwardian dress of yellow silk with mutton-chop sleeves and tiny pearl buttons, a picture hat covered with veiling and gold silk roses, and she was riding through town on a BSA 650 Gold Flash.

The main street of Foxton lay to the sun, broad as the back of a whale, normally so quiet that we got to know cars the way we recognised voices.

Our ears pricked at the piston slap of an A40, Mrs Meldrum coming in to get a dressing on her ulcer – and that was Dobby Baker's truck on its way to the Post Office Hotel. But in January, the beach filled up with aliens, people from Wellington and Palmerston North who got bored with sand and sea and came into the town to spend their money. They were different from us – not lah-de-dah, just different – and sometimes we felt embarrassed for them. They went into the Pacific Grill Room to ask for rare steak or raw oysters, or black coffee when all the restaurant coffee came from cans with milk mixed in. Or else the ladies wanted to know where the nearest restroom was, meaning lavatory, and we didn't know how to tell them there was only the one in the children's playground where you wouldn't go without gumboots.

On Friday nights the beach people took over the entire town. The streets were lined with Consuls and Zephyrs, Veloxes, Crestas, and a few of the posh ones, Daimler, Studebaker, Alvis Grey Lady, a new Austin Princess. Teenagers crowded the jukebox in the milkbar, spilling out the voices of Mario Lanza, Teresa Brewer and Patti Page. Men stood with children on the footpath, while their wives came into the chemist shop to buy bathing caps and other things.

Now, if a local woman wanted an item of a personal nature, she waited until the shop was empty or else passed a note across the counter. The holiday woman was different. She said in a loud voice, 'And a packet of Tampax, please.'

I took a box from under the counter and was about to wrap it, when she said, 'While I'm here, I'd better get a tube of Koromex cream.'

The shop was crowded. My face burned and words dried up. I opened the you-know-what drawer in front of a dozen pairs of eyes and took out a pink box. I was not sure how this stuff was used, but I knew why it was used. Everything in that drawer was associated with an activity that had no name except one too rude to repeat. Years ago, when my sisters and I first found out about it, we called it pompom. I don't know why. Pompom was what people did to get babies, and it was our own word. We could use it in public. Our parents didn't know what we meant or why we rolled about laughing.

Childish words have a habit of sticking. In moments of embarrassment, the you-know-what drawer became the pompom drawer.

Every Friday night, Mr Fetridge came in for his indigestion tablets. Mr Fetridge was an old and gentle widower with silver hair and a face like a seamed pumpkin, and although he shopped in the same places every Friday night, he always dressed in a suit with a bow tie and a flower in his buttonhole. 'Good evening. Awfully close, isn't it? Pending rain, I think. The tummy tablets, if you please.'

As I wrapped the tin, he put an extra half crown on the counter and asked for something else.

I didn't understand.

He repeated it, then, sensing my lack of comprehension, said, 'Perhaps you should fetch the chemist.'

I went into the dispensary and said to Mr Donnelly, 'Mr Fetridge wants, he said – French something or other –'

Without a word, my boss handed me the prescription he was filling, and went into the shop. I heard him open the pompom drawer. I heard more talk about the weather.

When he returned, Mr Donnelly told me matter-of-factly that French letter was another name for the male contraceptive Durex.

I didn't answer, or even look at him, but later I talked to Dulcie who worked in the shop. She was younger than me, but she had been working there for three years. 'He's old!' I told her. 'He – he's not even married!'

Dulcie raised her thin shoulders and let them drop with a sigh. 'Why don't you grow up?' she said.

That night I couldn't wait to tell my sister Joan what French letters were. I was disappointed to discover that she had known for years. The children used to bring them to school, she said, and blow them up over the tap to make water bombs. But I scored a hit when I told her who bought them.

'Mr Fetridge?' Her eyes widened and her tone became shrill. 'He's older than Dad. He must be over fifty!' Then her voice climbed to a squeak. 'He hasn't got a wife!'

I shrugged with immense satisfaction. 'What difference does that make?'

At 8.00 am the flax mills started up. The machine settled to a steady cry, wo-ow, wo-ow, wo-ow, as bunches of flax were fed through. The mouth of the stripper looked like the intake of a kitchen mincer, and if a man got his finger caught, it was off quick as a wink. Woolpack & Textiles paid generous compensation in case of accident, and there were two to three weeks off work. Still, a finger was a finger and it was a difficult decision for a man to make.

Wo-ow, wo-ow. Our parents were still in bed and I was able to read a Mickey Spillane novel at the breakfast table. My sister Heather took her time to cut her school lunch. She was fourteen, an attractive and good-natured girl with a big bust that spread the pleats of her gym frock. All she wanted from life was to get married and have lots of children. For as long as she can remember, she has been gathering names for babies: Violet and Pansy, Roland and Ruby, Hugh, Jimmy and Marigold.

Heather was not fond of school and she thought she might be getting a period pain.

'Take an AP Codeine,' I mumbled from the pages of *I, the Jury*.

'I feel really awful.' She tried to look the part, hoping I'd advise her to stay home. I ignored her and she went down the hall to wake up Mum.

We-ow. We-ow. We-ow.

My three sisters and brother were all younger than me. Joan, a pretty girl with sandy hair and freckles, was a nurse aide at Kimberley Hospital, Levin. Then there was Heather. Next came Barbara, a shy, dark nine-year-old who had Dad's tendency to rheumatic fever. Peter, at five, looked most like me except for his orange hair and green eyes.

Our mother's slippers sounded along the hall. Mickey Spillane was quickly replaced by a textbook, open at polysaccharides.

'Heather's staying home from school,' said Mum. 'She's got her monthlies.'

My sister caught my eye and said defensively, 'I'm not missing much. It's only sports.'

That explained everything. We all got sick on sports days. All the same, it was a wonder Mum didn't remember that Heather had the same ailment two weeks ago.

We-ow. The stripping mill was a quarter of a mile away, yet its singing filled the house.

Mum had in her hand the clock from the bedroom. 'Joy, you're going to be late for work. What's the matter with you? Been reading again? You'll get the sack, you will.'

It was true. I was late, late, so under the mattress with Mickey Spillane, out the door, buttoning my smock at the shoulder, onto my pushbike, blow, forgot to comb my hair, standing on the pedals, we-ow, we-ow, and now, in front of me, the clamouring of the nine o'clock school bell.

I knew I wouldn't be late if I had a motorbike.

We felt sorry for Mr Beaumont because his wife wouldn't let him drink. She had removed him from all temptation by shifting to Foxton

Beach and selling the car. He sat marooned in a house as dry as the sand dunes, and didn't go out except once a fortnight when she gave him a bus fare to go into Foxton to visit the doctor.

Mr Beaumont lived for that fortnightly visit. For thirteen days he was a dour man with a slack lower lip and a red face that ran downhill in lines of disappointment; but on the fourteenth day his eyes shone with recklessness. He always brought his prescription into the shop, wishing us a truly good day. 'I'll be off now to pay my social calls, you understand,' he said, twirling his hat by the brim. 'I'd be greatly obliged if one of you young ladies would acquaint me of the bus time, as usual.'

'Don't worry, Mr Beaumont. You can rely on us.'

He winked. 'If Mrs Beaumont should telephone, I'm still at the doctor's.'

'Of course, Mr Beaumont.'

We didn't know where he got the money for drink. Perhaps he relied on the generosity of his friends. Whatever, near the time for the 5.30 pm bus to the beach, Mr Beaumont was as happy as you please, and none too steady.

I walked across the road and pushed open the doors of the public bar. Cyril the barman waved a towel. 'Over there, the silly old bugger.'

Mr Beaumont was standing on a chair, reciting a poem about a dog with a limitless bladder. When he saw me he swallowed the rest of the verse and got down off the chair. He set his hat square on his head and drew a line with his eyes to the door. 'Thankee, my dear,' he said. 'Much obliged.' Then he charged across the bar with determination, and onto the street. I gave him his prescription and a small bag of peppermints, then helped him to his bus. He doffed his hat in a tidy farewell and found his usual seat behind the driver.

One day, we forgot.

It was time to close the shop and I was picking up the mats in the dispensary, ready to sweep out. The bus ground its gears past the door and Dulcie gave a cry. 'Mr Beaumont!'

I let the mats go. 'Mr Beaumont, we didn't –'

Mr Donnelly shook his head. 'You'd better go over and see if he's still there. All else failing, I'll run him home when I've finished.'

I went across the road and pushed through the crowded bar. Mr Beaumont was on a stool, asleep with his head on the bar near the till. Cyril mopped up around him. 'I tried to tell him it was bus time. Wouldn't believe me, the silly old drongo.'

I shook Mr Beaumont but he was as responsive as a large kapok mattress. 'Wake up! You've missed your bus. You have to go home.'

He peered at me with watering eyes and murmured, '– take you home again, Kathleen,' then he went back to sleep.

Artie Hines from the service station came over, glass of beer in hand. 'We just mended a tractor tyre, got to drop it off at the beach. We can give him a lift.'

'Would you really?'

'Too right. Got to get him home or his missus'll tear the town apart. Hey, you fellahs! Give us a hand, will you?'

Two men in overalls put down their glasses and came forward. They hooked Mr Beaumont under the arms and dragged him off the stool. Artie followed carrying Mr Beaumont's hat, and I followed Artie. Outside there was a grey truck with a tractor wheel on the back.

'Up you go, my beauty,' says Artie. 'You'll be as good as gold.'

As Mr Beaumont bounced onto the truck tray, he opened his eyes and smiled. Then, conducting with his hand over his chest, he sang, 'I'll take you home again, Kathleen, across the ocean far and wide.'

For an old man with emphysema, he sang remarkably well.

I gave Artie the prescription and explained what the peppermints were for.

'Bit late for that,' said Artie. 'He's dropped himself in the dunny this time, if you ask me.'

A moment later, Mr Beaumont's voice was lost in the roar of a tattered muffler and the truck bore him away down the main street, his feet hanging over the edge of the tray.

'He'll be for it,' said a knowing bystander.

Mr Beaumont didn't come into town again. His wife arranged for the doctor to make house calls and all prescriptions were sent out on the bus. Four months later, Mr Beaumont died in his sleep.

Cyril the barman came over to tell us the news. 'Poor old bugger,' he said, and he was crying.

My parents' marriage was often stormy, sometimes reaching hurricane force that needed intervention from a weary police constable on a bicycle.

We didn't like the rows but we understood them. Mum and Dad had the kind of romantic ideals that were portrayed on the cinema screen and were all too fragile for the harsh realities of sickness, poverty and a large family. It is true that for some people, adversity builds character, but for many it is destructive. My parents were not well equipped to deal with hardship and they suffered cruelly. But through the storms, the shouting and violence, their romance survived to blossom suddenly and beautifully as soon as the climate improved.

In spite of my father's deafness, they got a lot of pleasure from singing together. My mother had a huge voice of unrealised greatness. In different circumstances she could have been an operatic mezzo-soprano on the world stage. As it was, she drowned our church choir in splendid sound and filled the street with 'Gypsy Love Song' or 'Rose Marie' when hanging out the washing. My father's voice was pale by comparison but adequate, and on summer evenings they sat at the old harmonium and sang until they were hoarse. Dad's favourites were 'Annie Laurie', 'The Old Rugged Cross' and 'Whispering Hope'.

Sometimes we children were called to join in with our thin reedy voices, but none of us showed promise or enthusiasm. We were, after all, the generation of ready-made wireless music and this effort seemed unnecessary. Besides, our parents' singing was not really a family affair – something we sensed without understanding why. Their duets were a part of a larger overture.

Sometimes they left the harmonium to dance around the room, singing against each other with great affection. Then Dad stopped and glared at us. 'Away to ye'r beds!' he ordered. 'Ye'll be guid fer nothing come the morning. Did ye no hear? Away wi' ye!'

On cold winter evenings, the family gathered around the wood stove in the kitchen. The oven door was open and inside the oven were bricks that would later be put into socks, to warm our beds. Our parents sat with their feet in the opening of the oven. This was their privilege. The rest of us took up positions around the stove on a first-come, best-served basis and we sat reading, knitting, squabbling amongst ourselves in voices too low to attract a clout from either parent.

Sooner or later, the singing started. Dad dragged Mum onto his knee and put his arms around her waist. 'I love a lassie, a bonny, bonny lassie –'

Mum laughed and, reluctantly, I closed my book.

We were not allowed to waste power by burning lights in our bedrooms but if I departed early, I was able to snatch the torch unnoticed and read under the bedclothes. I took my brick from the oven and put it in a sock.

Dad sang, 'She's as sweet as the heather, the bonny purple heather –'

I went into the bedroom, arching my feet over the icy linoleum. Book and torch slid under the pillow, the brick was placed at the bottom of the bed.

Through the wall, I heard my father say, 'Time the rest of ye went tae ye byes.'

Above Me aged one year with my parents Peter and Cassia Summers.

Below The Summers family, 1952. Front row: Barbara, Joan, me.
 Back row: Heather, Cassia (Mum), baby Peter, Peter (Dad).

Above Ted and I with the
children at the farm, 1962.

Left With Sharon and Edward, Himatangi Beach, 1961.

Above Fish Bay, Kenepuru, RD2, Picton.

Below James and Malcolm with a shark, 1970s.

Above Malcolm and I in the bay, circa 1980.

Left Children's writers and illustrators in the Sounds, Fish Bay, Easter.

Above The old ladies of children's literature: (from left) Margaret Mahy, me, Dame Marie Clay and Dorothy Butler.

Below A job that comes with many hugs.

Above Reading to children during book week, New Zealand.

And my mother added, 'You heard your father. Do what you're told – this minute!'

There was a rule that we could not have boyfriends until we were eighteen. Joan and Heather considered this unfair, especially since our mother was married at eighteen, and I suspected from their giggles and whispers, and from the smell of cigarette smoke on their clothing, that their social experience went beyond the permitted bible class picnics and dances. I was greatly concerned for my sisters and more than a little envious. The restriction on boyfriends suited me because it gave me an excuse for being out of the pairing game. In truth, I was convinced that no interesting boy would look twice at me. Why should he? I didn't dress well. I didn't know how to dance. Dancing seemed to me a futile exercise and I didn't know why people did it.

I was not without experience of boys. I had been kissed three times – once outside the school gates when I was eleven, once at sixteen in the back of a car, and in a darkened street one night after church.

The most attractive thing about kissing was remembering it afterwards. At the time there were practical concerns that prevented enjoyment: getting noses in the way, trying to breathe, avoiding the clashing of teeth, wondering about spit and germs. But somewhere in the kiss there was a pleasure that became apparent afterwards, a small excitement that grew in solitude.

I had not had a boyfriend according to my parents' definitions, but I had been in and out of love since the age of four. Love was the condition that made, shaped and coloured my life. Love was all misery and all bliss, the inspiration behind nearly everything I learned and achieved. Love was pain. Love was enervating. Without it, I felt desperate.

Often love had been associated with some living person – adoration at a distance of favourite uncles or teachers, film actors Leslie Howard and Mel Ferrer. Sometimes the attachment had been to a character in a novel; sometimes to a long dead author or artist. I had been smitten by Robert Louis Stevenson and Frederic Chopin. Van Gogh would not have committed suicide had he met me. As for John Keats, well, there was the great love of my life. I remained faithful to him for two and a half years, pressing flowers between the pages of his poems, feeding on his sweet melancholy.

> Yes, I will be thy priest, and build a fane
> In some untrodden region of my mind,
> Where branched thoughts, new grown with pleasant pain,
> Instead of pines shall murmur in the wind.

This love I felt had nothing to do with sexual restlessness and that other business of making babies. Rather, it made itself felt above the waist. The head was full of it. It burned in the palms of the hands and was a weakness between the shoulder blades. It was a stammering of the heart, an aching in the lungs. But its true kingdom lay fair and square in the stomach. When love entered, it left a hole in the solar plexus so wide that the whole world seemed to pass through it.

Love was such a frequent visitor that it thought it owned me, and it would arrive without invitation. It was enough to see raindrops rolling on a cabbage leaf, or to observe the perfect dappling of colour on a cat's fur, to feel the beginnings of that yawning and yearning under the ribs.

Some nights, all too rarely, there was a marvellous dream that was filled with an emotion not experienced in waking. I was standing on a cliff above the sea. Behind me, there were white columns of a temple; in front there was blueness, blue sky down to blue sea, one element merging with the other. I dived from the cliff and discovered there was no skin between sky and water. I saw that the bottom of the ocean was covered with white marble paving stones, and there were white pillars similar to those on top of the cliff. I breathed easily as I swam between the pillars, looking for a marble staircase. My heart beat with an eager pain, for I knew that when I found the staircase, I would also find the golden man. Patches of light and shade shimmered on the whiteness, and my breath went before me in silver bubbles.

Then I saw the staircase and my chest ached with sweetness, for there was the man coming down the steps to meet me. His hands were outstretched and he smiled with such pleasure that clearly he had been waiting for me since the last dream. He was all gold. His hair floated behind him, his skin was polished metal. He swam with haste, reached for me, and then we were side by side, arms around each other, hips and legs touching. We floated like that – as though we were two people in a three-legged race. Gradually, his body passed into mine. He was absorbed through my skin until he was totally within me, shining gold through my skin. In that moment of extraordinary pleasure, I was the man and he was also me.

I always woke up feeling golden and content. I did not know enough to ask myself what the dream meant.

Our parents managed to keep their daughters in an innocence we later relabelled *ignorance* for more years than they probably intended, and I had been at school for several years before I discovered the difference between girls and boys.

I knew there was a difference. I just didn't know what it was, apart from the fact that girls had long hair and dresses, while boys had trousers and hair cut short. Mum told us that mothers went to the hospital and waited for angels to bring them babies from heaven. That was clear. But all babies had short hair and long gowns. So how did the mothers know if they had girls or boys?

The question became more significant when I began school and realised how different boys were in their appearance, their play and the way teachers treated them. At six years of age, I decided that the person who should have the answer was my own mother. So I asked her. 'How do mothers know the difference between girl and boy babies?

Mum must have assumed that I knew and was being clever, for she smacked me across the ear and snapped, 'Don't be rude!'

I backed away, holding the side of my head. Rude? Rude was something to do with bottoms.

I didn't ask again, but the mystery was resolved a year or so later when I stayed with relatives in Auckland and was taken to the museum. At a bend in the stairs of the Auckland Museum was a bronze cherub, completely naked. It looked a bit like my sisters and me, except there was something sticking out under the belly. I leaned over the stair rail until I could touch it, and afterwards, found excuses to run up and down those stairs so that I could repeat the experience. Some instinct in me came to life and filled the gaps in my knowledge.

So this was what a boy looked like without his clothes!

How funny and silly! How delicious!

Because the pharmacy was the only one in town, it had to offer twenty-four-hour service. I could earn extra for my bike by looking after the dispensary while my boss was away for the evening. Only a handful of people came to the side door, so I spent most of the time copying the day's prescriptions into the register, tidying the dispensary or studying my chemistry textbooks. I could also do chemistry experiments, provided they didn't leave residual odours of rotten eggs.

Late one night there was a heavy knocking on the side door. When I opened it, I saw a man who could have stumbled directly out of the graveyard in *Great Expectations*. He had been cut and bruised about the face, had startled eyes and was shaking. He stared about the dispensary. He was just out of prison, he said, and his nerves were bad. Could I give him something to make him sleep?

I explained that I was not able to do that.

He snatched up a bottle of Digoxin. What about those?

I told him they were for heart disease. Then I suggested he went down the road to Dr Malthus and got a prescription.

No, no, no. He grasped the edge of the dispensary bench to still his trembling hands, and told me to phone the doctor. Now, he insisted. Phone now. He pushed me towards the phone and watched closely while I made the call.

Dr Malthus' voice was measured and careful. He said he would come at once, but in the meantime, I was to give the man a script for seven Nembutal.

I counted the capsules into a glass phial and asked the man to sign the prescription form while I wrote the label. 'The doctor's coming to see you,' I told him.

Without a word, the man took the top off the pill phial, tipped all the capsules into his mouth and threw the empty container on the floor. He grabbed the stock bottle of Nembutal, pushed it into his pocket and then stumbled out into the night.

When Dr Malthus arrived, he found me distraught, for I believed that the man intended to kill himself. The doctor shook his head and told me a little about drug addiction.

I was appalled to learn that the means of healing could itself cause sickness. Was there nothing purely good in the world? I went home, somehow feeling responsible for a tattered man with panic in his eyes.

Boyfriends were one thing. Friends who were male, were another. I had always had as many male friends as female, and of all ages, but now there was a small group in their late teens whom I cultivated with shameless assiduity. They were, of course, the owners of motorbikes.

My parents – with that uncanny knowing that parents have – knew that there was no nonsense about these friendships and I was free to go to George's or Allen's on a Saturday afternoon and mess about with bikes.

The boys were accommodating. If I helped them to clean their machines, to sand down frames ready for painting, rinse out chains in petrol, clean carburettors, cut new cork gaskets, then I could have the occasional ride. Once I got an AJS for a whole afternoon. The boys were having races on Foxton Beach. I was given the bike and left at the fork in the road to watch for traffic cops. If a patrol car took one route to the beach, I was to race down the other and warn the boys. But the reckless ride was not to be. There was no sign of the law and I sat at the intersection for more than three hours before I was released from sentry duty.

Allen was eighteen and had compulsory military training coming up. He had hinted that I might be able to look after his Gold Flash while he was in camp at Linton. I clung to the hope, but there was a recent problem. Allen had a girlfriend who disapproved of me. While we were working in the garage, she watched from the doorway, talking to Allen and giving me cold looks. She had told Allen that she didn't want me going around there any more.

I could still visit George but his bike was an old Indian, not far off the junk heap. It was a battle for me to get it off the rest, and with all that compression, I usually ended up standing on top of the kickstart, like an idiot.

It was Allen's machine that I wanted. I bent scruples and added to my prayers the earnest plea that Allen would get rid of his girlfriend before he went into army camp.

I had a number of casual evening and weekend jobs, and my total earnings over the months were good for someone my age. Yet my savings barely grew. My parents were right. I was not good with money. My dreams of a bike were threatened by numerous extravagances, books mainly, a 35 mm camera, materials for drawing and painting, a microscope and subscriptions to two motorcycle magazines. I was constantly disgusted at my lack of thrift.

One afternoon in September, my father came into the pharmacy, wearing the widest of grins. 'I've got ye a bike,' he announced.

I came out from behind the counter. He wasn't joking. He meant it. He'd bought me a motorbike.

'Ye can pay me back,' he said. 'It wasna cheap, mind ye. Near on sixty quid.'

Sixty pounds? George's old Indian was worth more than that.

Dad led me out of the shop and proudly indicated a machine propped against the kerb. It was a toy! It was a little old toy! He'd bought a 1949 Royal Enfield 147 cc with a hand gear change aligned against the petrol tank and a rubber-bulb hooter.

I couldn't ride a thing like that!

He yanked it off the stand and kicked it over. It came to life with a high-pitched cackle.

I knew what Dad had done. He was afraid I'd buy something big and dangerous so he'd got in first with this – this –

My eyes filled with tears.

He misread my emotion. 'Aye, I knew ye'd like it,' he said.

After work, I took the bike around to Allen's place. 'It's only temporary,' I told him, 'something to get me from A to B while I'm saving for a decent bike.'

Allen folded up with laughter. 'You look as though you are running on a couple of castors.'

I rode off in a sulk.

It was a rotten little bike and I hated it. The humiliation of puttering around on a half-grown machine drove me into deep misery, but I tried to conceal my feelings from Dad who truly believed that he had made all my dreams come true.

On Saturday, I put on a heavy coat and gloves, wound a scarf around my neck, fitted on a pair of old flying goggles, and rode out of Foxton. It was not much of a bike but I might as well try it out on a longer ride.

The engine went into a high-pitched scream as I opened up the throttle on the Himatangi straight. I let go of the handlebars and rocked the tank with my knees, feeling the bike respond with one gentle arc after another. It did 65 mph flat out. My hair flapped like a rag, my cheeks blew out, water streamed back from my eyes under the goggles. I put my head back and gave a long yodelling cry that scarcely rose above the racing engine.

In that moment, the road lifted under the wheels, the trees flung back their arms and the whole world shouted with laughter.

Reflection can colour experience, and at the time of writing this, I am not sure what dulled my passion for motorbikes. It could have been that I was doomed to a little two-stroke because I never did save enough for the machine of my dreams; or it could have been that in the third year of my apprenticeship, I met a beautiful man who was learning to fly, and that led to a whole new story. After my first flight in a Tiger Moth I was like Toad from *The Wind in the Willows*, who sat dazed in the road, denouncing canary yellow carts. Nothing was quite as exciting as sitting in an open cockpit of a biplane that seemed as light and mobile as a butterfly. A motorcycle became nothing more than a means of getting me to the Middle Districts Aero Club for flying lessons.

In 1956 there still existed a 50 per cent government subsidy for students learning to fly. With World War II still fresh in the collective memory, the subsidy was intended to train pilots who would be on standby for the Air Force if needed. In spite of the precedent set by Jean Batten and a few other women pilots, I don't think it occurred to anyone that a girl might want to fly. At Middle Districts Aero Club, I was the only one in a large group of male students, and while at first I was a little nervous about this, I soon discovered that I was in a large family of big brothers who were kind, respectful and encouraging. Most of them had careers in sight, wanting to move on to commercial licences and jobs as airline or topdressing pilots. Already, many of the Tiger Moth aircraft in New Zealand had become part of topdressing fleets, reconstructed so that the second cockpit became the fertiliser hopper. The three DH 82s in the Middle Districts Club were viewed with affection and contempt by most of the career students, who were keen to get to the Cessnas, Pipers, and then dual engines. They saw nothing exciting about a biplane that cruised at 48 mph. But for me, the Tiger was pure poetry made flesh – or rather, wood and canvas. The open cockpit, slow speed, the sensitivity of a fully aerobatic plane, were marvellous. I had no ambition to fly anything else.

There was always a chivalrous knight on hand to swing the prop and remove the chocks. Cockpit checks were very simple: trim, mixture, fuel, flaps, ignition, harness and hatches, and we were away, trundling along the grass runway. Now, 78 mph seems an unbelievable take-off speed, yet when the stick came back the plane lifted into the air like a bird.

I went solo in the usual time, about five hours, and joined in club activities like cross-country flights and dawn raids that involved dropping flour bombs on neighbouring clubs in Whanganui and Masterton.

All weekend work, and likewise study, got cancelled when the weather was good enough for flying. Nothing was more important than this.

I flew all three Tigers in the Club fleet, but my favourite was ZK-BFA, and when I booked in the instructor would try to reserve it for me. This was the aircraft I badly damaged in a ground loop.

It happened on a fine Sunday morning after days of heavy rain. The bright breeze meant a chance to practise wheel landings. These were engine-forced landings for windy conditions, instead of the usual three-pointer.

'Keep away from the area behind the control tower,' Claude Baines the instructor told me. 'The ground there is very swampy.'

Away I went, circuit after circuit, landing with power on two wheels and then dropping throttle and tail skid. There was the usual Sunday crowd outside the Club, and since there were no airline flights out of Milson in those days, all I had to do was watch out for other small aircraft. But in doing so, I forgot the instructions about the wet ground behind the control tower.

I touched down and the wheels dug in. Water, grass, mud, flew past me, and then bits of prop, as the plane tumbled over onto its back. Before I was aware of what had happened, I was hanging upside down in the harness. I heard a steady drip, drip, and could smell fuel. I shut off the switches, pulled the pin in my harness and fell headfirst into swamp.

The first cars from the Club arrived on the scene as I crawled out from under the plane, my flying helmet and goggles covered in mud. People asked if I was all right. I wasn't the slightest bit hurt but when I tore off the goggles and saw the damage done to ZK-BFA, I felt dreadful. This lovely aircraft that had companioned me was in ruins. I had gone solo in her, done countless circuits and bumps, had leaned out of her in an attempt to drop a bag of flour on a flight instructor's sports car. I'd heard the wind singing in her wires when I'd stalled her at 5000 ft and then kicked her over into a spin, seen horizons come up over her tail in a loop. Now she lay on her back, tailplane torn off, wings shredded, propeller reduced to a stub. How could I ever forgive myself?

Everyone was kind and very gentle. Claude Baines took me to his home where his wife gave us lunch, and then I was back at the airport and into the air. I didn't want to go up. Claude insisted: 'If you fall off a horse, you get straight back on.'

What was left of BFA had been dragged into the hangar. ZK-BFG had been wheeled out and I was guided to it. One circuit with Claude and I was on my own again, one wheel landing after another. It was all right. Yes, I could do it.

But I never did get my private pilot's licence. The next year I was married and pregnant, and the young woman who could do stunts on a motorbike or throw a Tiger Moth around the skies could not stand on a chair. The hormonal changes designed to protect a baby do not compromise and I, like many other mothers, became very sensitive to risk. The word *danger* becomes instinct to the pregnant woman.

Did I miss flying? Yes, and I still do at times. But what replaced it gave a fulfilment I could not have imagined.

Children

Those who spend time cruising in the Marlborough Sounds know that charts and knowledge of land configuration are essential to navigation. But there must also be understanding of the influence of the moon, magnetic poles and weather. Yachties will read the curdled cloud in the morning and the yellow sky at sunset, and adjust their journey to a wind that will rip the tops off waves, or pounce down from the hills in several directions at once. They know not to edge into a shallow harbour on an ebbing tide. The days after full moon, they watch the flotsam on the tide lines for submerged logs. Fishermen accept that mankind is the only creature without a natural feeding pattern, and when cows and sheep are grazing, the fish will also be biting.

But nature has patterns even more mysterious and it is only when we have a lifetime of experience behind us that we appreciate the currents that cannot be named but are known by the consistency of their effect. They are the currents of paradox. What we once saw in life as gain, becomes loss. The loss that we would have avoided, is actually gain.

We learn to trust these tides. Experience tells us that when we have finished a class in Life School, we are moved on to the next. The chart we've tightly clutched is taken away and a larger one put in its place. And those of us who have always longed for calm waters learn how growth comes through storms. It seems that tension is essential for increase. It's a law of nature and how we begin life. One little cell divides in two. It divides again and again and again. Growth means movement, rupture, division, leaving something behind to come to a new place of development, and that is usually accompanied by some kind of discomfort. Whatever our close view of such transitions, when we look back at them from a distance, we see that they were exactly right.

In July 1956 I became pregnant. A feeling of fullness came soon after conception, a knowledge that flooded every part of the body like some hefty injection of euphoria. It was hormonal, of course, but what a change it wrought. I was like a ship becalmed and happy to be so, sitting on my own reflection, sails slack, life gently lapping against me.

There could have been speculation about a future that was dark for motorcycling, flying and pharmacy exams. At that stage there was no prospect of marriage. My parents didn't know and would surely disown me when they found out. I would have no income. But those considerations didn't matter. In a knowledge that was as old as the earth, I had discovered what this solid clumsy body was made for, and there was a conviction that I would do this well.

The energetic nineteen-year-old who woke early to plan her day and was always leaning forward to the next thing, had gone. I hugged a new name to myself. Mother. The desire to write and draw had also disappeared. It was as though this one act of creation was enough.

I was a treasure chest holding the most beautiful thing in the world.

A few weeks later, the pregnancy was confirmed by our family doctor. He looked anxious. 'Do you want to go through with it?' he asked.

I could not believe what I was hearing. My baby! My lovely baby!

'Yes!' I cried. 'Oh yes, yes, yes!'

'If I were you, I wouldn't tell your mother and father,' he said. 'Not yet.'

He wrote details on the patient index card, in Greek. 'That's so my receptionist won't be able to read it,' he explained.

He need not have worried. When I left the surgery I went straight to Ross's drapery store next door to the pharmacy, and bought two maternity bras.

Within a couple of days, the whole town knew.

In spite of his early misgiving, Ted, the baby's father, married me three months later, and I moved with my possessions, four tea chests of books, to the Cowley farm in Whakarongo near Palmerston North. My new name was appropriate. Cowley literally means dairy farm, and in this green valley we milked a herd of seventy Jerseys – elegant cows with fine bones, large udders, soft eyes. We had the old style of milking shed and as my belly grew, I needed to squat with knees wide apart to put the machines on the animals, who knew what it was all about.

The following April, a beautiful baby girl, plump and fair, face like a newly opened rose, was born with short labour and minimum effort. The next year a son with a mop of dark hair and huge appetite came into the world. The year after that, there was another daughter, active from birth and eyes full of wisdom. Fifteen months later, we had a son who smiled almost from birth and was adored by the others. In a short time we had been given four children who filled us with awe and gratitude.

The young man who had dreaded fatherhood became a splendid dad. Although Ted was nervous with small babies, once our children showed signs of becoming people, he bonded with them to become a loving and exciting father and friend.

For as long as I could remember, I had enjoyed the company of my younger siblings, and the children in my care at a Presbyterian Sunday school. But nothing in my experience had prepared me for the attachment I would feel for my own children. I was besotted.

I'd read books on mothering and childcare, but instinct discarded most of the rules. If a baby cried, he or she was picked up. A hungry baby was fed whatever the hour. Awake or asleep, the baby was seldom alone in the bedroom cot, but with me – lying in the clothes basket while I did the ironing, tied into a shawl when I walked down the farm to change the electric fence. At milking time, the baby was in a carrycot in the dairy, while the others played in a sandpit built for them on the other side of the yard rails. When the first lot of cows let down their milk, mine would come too, and if I were on my own I'd have to switch the machines off so I could go into the dairy and feed the baby. All this appeared very primitive to some people with traditional ideas about baby discipline and hygiene; and now, half a century later, I could have a more cautious view of waking toddlers late at night so they could go out to see the stars and, on hot days, letting them run naked. Ted and I dressed up in each other's clothes to 'buy things' from a shop the children had set up in their bedroom. We allowed preschoolers to sleep on the lawn at night in cardboard boxes – because they wanted to – and showed them how to warm their feet in a fresh cowpat.

Ted and I were very young, in our early twenties, and our enjoyment of our children was endless. He made them bubble pipes, rubber-band guns, wooden puzzles, showed them how to create rockets with old

plastic syringes and firecrackers. I bought end rolls of newsprint, crayons and paint and we drew pictures every day. We told stories and jokes. We trooped in to the library every Friday night. Our meals were usually on a table littered with plasticine and fragments of playdough.

My mentor and friend in all this was Ted's aunt Triss Ranford, who lived at the back of the farm. She was a teacher who had five boys and was very active in Playcentre. It was Triss who gave me the courage to do what I felt best for the children rather than conform to the attitudes of the day which saw children as adult possessions, adult investment. When my children talk about those idyllic times, I don't think they fully appreciate how much came from the example of their Great-Aunt Trissie.

Times have changed; now most parents enter the world of their children in much the same way as we did, and will readily identify with this. The advice I would give those new to the prospect of parenthood is simple: the most important thing is to enjoy your children. Give them your time. Everything else will fall into place.

No one can look into the eyes of a newborn baby without seeing eternity. Children seem to come into the world bearing wisdom as ancient as the universe and until this becomes buried under layers of social conditioning, they can sometimes speak truth that startles us.

I am often amazed at statements from four- and five-year-old children who view the world with direct simplicity.

When our oldest son Edward was four we visited my father, who was then living on his own. By Dad's bed was an ashtray with the three proverbial monkeys perched on its edge – see no evil, hear no evil, speak no evil. Edward, a very practical child, wanted to know what these monkeys were doing, and as he pointed to the monkey with its hands over its eyes, I tried to explain. 'This little monkey can't see bad things.'

Edward frowned deeply. 'But Mum, he wouldn't be able to see *anything!*'

I stared at him. My son the teacher!

For several years we had a weekly family conference at which we could all have a say without anyone else interrupting. The usual subjects were school, pocket money, house and farm chores and what was just or unjust, as well as suggestions for the Sunday afternoon outing when we went out for a family drive before milking. But other topics came up: one of the older children wanted to know what happened when people died. Before I could offer some of the traditional answers, Judith, aged five, cut in: 'We get borned again.'

I said, 'Why do you think that?'

She shrugged. 'The sun goes round and round. The moon goes round and round. The world goes round and round. Everything goes round and round. We do, too.'

I looked into her gorgeous eyes, calm and full of knowing, and thought, Yes, and you have been round and round many times.

Almost all my life, I have been learning from children, and I owe much to literally thousands of teachers who have welcomed me into their classrooms. Because adults control all aspects of children's book production, classroom research has always been important to me, especially when I'm writing for emergent readers. Five-year-olds are not reflective, and it would be a waste of time to ask them what they thought about being five. But I can go into a class of eight- and nine-year-olds and tap into their memories of being five – memories that are still fresh. Because they are safely removed from that age, they don't hesitate to give me the information I am seeking. This has happened in different countries; and whatever the fashions of time and culture, the world of childhood is much the same. Children have the same feelings about their position in the family. They fear the dark. They hate being laughed at. They resent going to bed early and dislike strong-flavoured food. They find tears, tummy-buttons and big toes interesting. They love to laugh, and enjoy slapstick humour. Their ambitions are to whistle, do up shoelaces, sit in the car without a babyseat and watch a scary movie.

But often children will say something that gets carved into my memory. There was the six-year-old boy, face wrinkled in a frown, who urgently needed to ask a question: 'Hey, Joy, how come you like little kids?'

I looked at his small worried face and felt the pain of the experience that had taught him big people did not like little people.

At a school near Las Vegas, I was doing a writing workshop with children aged nine and ten, many of them Native American. One handsome Navajo boy, with thick black hair and soft eyes, came to me while the others were writing. He said, 'I can't read and write.'

I sat him down beside me. 'Do you want to tell me how you feel about that?'

He nodded. 'When I try to write I stand outside of myself.'

I knew exactly what he meant. Reading and writing made him feel inauthentic. He came from an oral tradition. Story was something that came from people, not from books and pens. So I asked him if he would like to tell me a story. He was a bit shy at first, but then told me how his little brother got sick and his aunty sang to him and made him better. His aunt, I gathered, was a medicine woman. I wanted to borrow that story but couldn't. It belonged to him and it needed his voice.

A charming story told to me by the mother of a four-year-old boy, was a reminder of the clear vision of the young child. The grandmother of this child had made him his first pair of big boy pyjamas, and she gave the package to him when the family met for Sunday dinner. The boy could not wait to try them. He put the pyjamas on and paraded around the living room to show everyone. Suddenly, he stopped in front of his mother, looked down and said, 'What's this?'

His mother replied, 'That's a fly.'

The child looked disappointed. 'Oh,' he said. 'I thought it was a penis hole.'

Sometimes I have stored memories that served no purpose except to cut me down to size. Many years ago, I was telling stories in a small country school north of Levin. In front of me sat a red headed boy who had extraordinary focus. His eyes and mouth were three circles of attention, and when it came to question time, his was the first hand up. 'How long did it take you to write *A Lion in the Meadow*?'

I explained, 'I didn't write *A Lion in the Meadow*. That's Margaret Mahy's book.'

His eyes opened wider. 'You mean you're not Margaret Mahy?'

His disappointment was so great that I still feel twinges of guilt.

When our youngest son James was nearly two, I became pregnant. Ted and I were both pleased. Another perfect addition to the clan! Our excitement grew as we did up the battered pushchair and sorted baby clothes. I started knitting little garments, needles clicking as we listened to the *Goon Show* on the kitchen radio. Ted worked out that the child would be born in winter when the cows were dry and he could probably be at the hospital with me for the birth.

My mother's oldest sister Esther, who loved babies, had looked after our older three when James was born. She was overjoyed that another was on the way and would be with us again. She too started knitting.

In the fifteenth week of pregnancy, I was feeding out silage when I felt stomach cramps. I knew there was nothing to worry about. After all, I was strong and healthy and good at having babies.

The next morning I woke up in a pool of blood.

Ted offered practical comfort. 'There'll be another,' he said.

But there wasn't. For some unknown reason, I did not conceive again.

Seasons of Partnership

Plato wrote in his *Symposium* of quadruped humans who displeased the gods and were cut in half. On two feet, the punished were forced to wander the earth searching for their other self.

The story can apply to some aspects of relationship but it suggests that we need to be completed by partners who are the same as us, whereas most of us choose people who are complementary. And anyway, I don't think Plato was talking about the friendship we call 'platonic'. In the context of *The Symposium*, he meant, essentially, physical union. These days, we have adapted Plato's name for a wider sphere of relationship that is probably best described by the Buddhist saying, 'When the pupil is ready the teacher will arrive'. Only the Buddhists are not talking in metaphor but literal truth. It is how the universe works. Human beings complete each other. We are each other's teachers.

Outside of school and formal education, most of my teachers have been men. The first was my father. The skills considered feminine – cooking, knitting, crochet, sewing – were picked up at a young age from my mother, grandmothers and aunts. It was Dad, with damaged heart valves that made him breathless, who took me beyond the gender barrier and instructed me in work usually kept for boys. He knew what had to be done but couldn't do it, so I learned to hold a hammer at the end of the handle, to measure twice, cut once, and stand directly over a saw to get the cut straight. He taught me to use a soldering iron, a chisel and plane, to resole shoes on a last, chop wood, paint and wallpaper, mend a fuse, change a tyre and make a simple bookcase – all valuable life skills.

That was the beginning. An ongoing gift was a long line of male friends who introduced me to motorbikes, flying, yachting, bushcraft, farming, fishing boats, woodturning; who shared their knowledge of classical music, world religions, law, economics, astronomy.

In effect, the influence of these men has built a practical extension to a creative mind, and I have no doubt whatsoever, it was their gift of disciplined thinking that made me a writer. Without such influence, my writing would probably have gone no further than Technicolor bursts of self-indulgence.

My brain was Plato's severed quadruped. Male friends have introduced it to its other half.

Most of us do find that special person who is friend, teacher, lover, partner all in one, and even if it is only for a season, the influence of that person remains with us always. Some find it more than once. For me it has happened three times and each in the right season of life.

The years of my first marriage were a time of exuberant spring growth. Ted and I were children with our children, and although we worked long hours on the farm, the work was part of physical fulfilment. The kind of satisfaction that some get from marathons or a session at the gym, we got from heaving hay bales onto a trailer, milking, cleaning the shed, feeding calves and shifting stock. Frost-filled nights were part of springtime, as were summer afternoons with the herd moving slowly through dust and flies.

Housework too, was often physical celebration: cleaning the old coal range and polishing the top with blacking until it shone; standing by the stove with towels as four golden bodies, glistening with soap, ran squealing from the bathroom to the warmth of the fire.

On Mondays, the copper was lit to wash the clothes, beginning with the whites, sheets, towels, nappies and ending with the farm work trousers scrubbed on a washboard. One of my early stories published by the *Home Journal* began: 'It was a fine day, Monday, washing day, a bright explosion of a day with a Reckitt's Blue sky full of scudding suds and an outsize wind that ballooned the shirts and pyjama pants.'

I expect that would have little meaning for a generation with automatic washing machines and driers.

As a child I never felt young. I had learned that life was serious and a minute wasted was lost forever. I am greatly indebted to Ted and our lovely children for giving me back a laughing childhood.

Ted also introduced me to my own body. It was he who surprised me with the discovery of sexual pleasure, and in those years we fell together so easily. A walk down the farm to get the cows, an accidental brushing of arm and leg – and it was over the fence and into the long grass, and oops, another baby.

Ted taught me that the world was not going to stop if I occasionally ignored my bone-deep Scottish work ethic. I thought he and I would play in springtime forever, and when the marriage ended it seemed that my life was also at an end.

It was a few years before I learned that an ending is also another beginning, and what happened was meant to be.

The summer season of maturity came with my 1971 marriage to Malcolm Mason. This was not a feverish falling headfirst into love, but a deep liking that wound itself around us until we were bound together, a part of each other's life.

I knew Malcolm as the president of PEN. He had written two books about his war experiences, and his name appeared occasionally with feature articles in newspapers. During 1969 I received several postcards from him from various parts of the world. *I know a Polish translator who could be interested in translating your novel.* Another time: *I'd like to have a chat with you about your writing.* But because he always signed these notes, *Yours sincerely, M J Mason*, I did not suspect that he was trying to attract my attention. I didn't reply, partly because I was busy, but also because I wasn't keen on some aspects of the social web that surrounded writers. Frustrated by the silence, Malcolm had the good sense to get in his car on New Year's Day 1970, and drive to Palmerston North. He brought with him a picnic hamper with tomatoes and lettuce from his garden.

That was a pleasant surprise. During the years on my own, there had been a few men who had wanted to 'talk about writing'. Usually, there were invitations to dinner at a restaurant. I sometimes accepted on the condition that I paid for my own meal. When there was protest, I explained why it was important for me to pay my own way. The men would be aggrieved, angry – or both. How could I insult them by imagining such a thing? But they never asked me out again.

Malcolm was different. We sat on the bank of the Pohangina River, watching families splashing in the water, eating sandwiches and drinking tea from a thermos. He was chivalrous, respectful, an entertaining conversationalist and funny. When he dropped me back at my flat, he kissed me on the cheek and said he would phone. He did. He phoned that night. And the next day, and the next. We were in contact every day after that, until he died in 1985.

As the friendship blossomed, Malcolm sent frequent telegrams to the pharmacy where I worked as a dispensary assistant. These telegrams relayed songs, one line at a time. *I'll be loving you always. With a love that's true always.* The shop girls thought this was very romantic and when a telegram arrived, they were in front of me, bright-eyed, waiting to hear the next episode of an unfolding love story.

In March 1970, on Himatangi Beach, Malcolm tried to propose. 'I don't suppose a girl like you could possibly –'

'Yes,' I replied.

'Do you mean that you would – that you – you could –'

'Yes, yes!'

At that stage I was confident of the friendship, and because Malcolm was nearly twenty-five years older than me, I was also sure that he wouldn't leave me for a younger woman. We married in a Wellington registry office with Malcolm's lifelong friends John and Katharine Robson in attendance, and after the short ceremony, I suggested we go back home to open a bottle of champagne. I was surprised that Malcolm wanted to have a cup of tea in a small café. Only when we got back to the house did I understand why. The delay was to allow his office staff time to finish filling our home with flowers. I had never seen so much spring blossom. He'd bought every bloom in the florist's shop, and they crammed all containers – vases, bowls, saucepans, kitchen sink, laundry buckets, even the bath and toilet – the house overflowing with the sweetness of daffodils, freesias, carnations, narcissi, violets, stock, anemones and ranunculi.

Malcolm was a man of extravagant romantic gestures. He was also a person of great integrity and uncompromisingly honest, which meant that people either loved him or hated him. A chartered accountant, he was in demand internationally as a 'troubleshooter', sent to collect debts or to rescue businesses that were failing due to poor management and/or staff extravagance. It was a job he did well, but at times, it didn't earn him friends.

The four Cowley children adored him. He was a caring stepfather and very entertaining. He enlarged the children's education with travel around the Pacific, had the girls enrolled at Queen Margaret College, and thrilled the boys with his unending supply of war stories. Edward and James particularly liked the story of the time the young Captain Mason escaped German capture by diving into a river. He'd told the German officer in the car that he had to stop for a call of nature. When he was let out of the car, the officer accompanied him to the riverbank at the side of the road.

'Did you really have a pee?' Edward asked.

'No,' said Malcolm. 'I was so scared I couldn't find it.'

Another time, Malcolm escaped by jumping off a train, an incident that left him with a permanently damaged knee. During the months on the run in Italy, he had chronic dysentery and pneumonia, both of which left ongoing weakness.

Although the war stories were forthcoming, he was very reticent about awards. We had been married for several years when an envelope arrived addressed to Lt Col. M. J. Mason MC, OBE. I thought this was a practical joke from one of his friends, but Malc shook his head and looked rather embarrassed.

I said, 'You didn't tell me you had an OBE!'

He shrugged. 'That stands for Other Buggers' Efforts.'

Malcolm was very supportive of my writing. He was also a kind friend to Ted, who used to phone him occasionally for financial advice. The children and I saw him as a man of intrinsic goodness, larger than life, generous, quick-moving, quick-tempered, and very funny.

I remember him rebuking me for something, as he went out the back door. Before I could call out a response, his face was against the kitchen window, making absurd kissing gestures on the glass. What could I say to that?

Once, when he came in from the garden and sat down to lunch, Sharon and Judith pointed out a large green caterpillar crawling on his shirt. Malcolm calmly plucked off the caterpillar, put it in his mouth and ate it. The girls screamed and Malc smiled. 'It's only cabbage with skin around it,' he said.

Malcolm's sense of humour never left him. It bubbled up through the darkest times of chemotherapy and sometimes shocked visitors who were not prepared for someone who could make jokes about death.

A few days before he died, I was sitting on the bed with him watching a rerun of his favourite comedy, *Dad's Army*. Malc took my hand, patted it and said, 'Remember all those buggers who said our marriage would never last? Well, they were right.'

We kept Malcolm at home during the last weeks of his life, and although he was too ill to cope with people, he looked forward to seeing his friend Terry Coles who sat with him nearly every morning. I was grateful for these visits that allowed me to attend to housework or do a bit of shopping. I saw Terry as a quiet, gentle fellow, the most understated man I had ever met, and I knew Malcolm responded to his peace-filled presence.

After Malcolm's death in July 1985, Terry kept in touch and four years later, when I was living in the Sounds, he phoned to ask if I would marry him. I agreed on two conditions: that he talk to a counsellor and that he go on a retreat to discern if this was right for him. Terry was a priest and although he was not a man to make rash decisions, I wanted to be sure that he wasn't doing something he would later regret.

Terry did as I requested, and came back to me certain that he wanted to get married. He also warned me that we would get some criticism within the Church, and we did weigh that in our decision. As it happened, we received warm, supportive letters and phone calls from Catholic priests and religious. Some lay people were upset, but everything else in our experience affirmed our decision; and what has flowed from our marriage since, makes us aware that together we have achieved far more than the sum of our independent work. In partnership, we've produced four books of reflections – Terry's photos, my writing, the one inspiring the other in no set order. Terry sees with an inner eye sensitive to beauty and harmony. In his photographs, he makes people look like flowers, and flowers like people.

Ours is the autumn partnership, a time of ripeness and dissemination, of giving out from the fullness we give each other. The deep and quiet friendship brings a feeling of completion to our lives. We talk little, touch often, seek each other's company and find pleasure in our complementary roles. At the end of the day we complete the *Dom Post* cryptic crossword together. Separately, we get less than half of it done. We spend time preparing good food and have the same taste in wine. We go to sleep holding hands.

And what of the winter season? We don't know, but assume that when the frosts of age come, winter will be a solo journey, one carrying the spirit of the other. What we both know is that winter is not the season of death, but preparation for a time of great growth.

Fishing in the Dark

Fishing in the bay on a calm night is an exquisite experience. The torch makes a small circle of light on a road congealed in wet bush fragrance, earth, rotting leaves, hints of bird and animal, scent of gum leaves pierced by the sweetness of cabbage tree flowers, the smell of the old karaka tree that hangs over the upturned dinghy.

Of recent years my boat has been an inflatable with a metal bottom, easy to drag down to the water, stable for someone with arthritic knees. It has long oars. 'Why do you want oars this length?' they asked in the boat shop. They don't know how the wind can sweep into our bay, and how oars can be effective brakes in those sudden gusts. Besides, I don't like the noise of an outboard when I go fishing, and neither do the snapper. Long oars are fast, relatively quiet.

The sky is freckled with stars that make milky spots in the black water. I switch off the torch so that my eyes can adjust to starlight and the phosphorescent fireworks that drip from the blades. The hills around the bay are outlined with black tree shapes and I line up a particular old pine to find my fishing place. The torch goes on again and it attracts garfish. They plop around the dinghy in fire-green circles. I put a hand line over and allow the boat to quietly drift away from it. Usually there is a snapper or two, but fresh fish for breakfast is only the excuse. I sit out on the water at night to feed my soul.

Dawn starts with blackness turning grey, and the stars retreat into a void. Towards Kenepuru Head, the horizon turns yellow as a solitary bellbird starts up the choir. Within minutes the bay is echoing with silvery chimes, and light is spreading itself over water as smooth as green glass.

Years ago Sharon, in the sixth form, asked me to make her a velvet jacket for her Queen Margaret ball. 'I want it in Sounds green,' she said and I knew exactly what colour she meant.

The sun rises higher. Two shags fly past, their wings almost touching their reflections. The trees and ferns on the bank are duplicated upside down in the water. But I know the sky has promised wind, and here it is in my face, a little breeze that makes the perfect pictures in the sea abstract, trees shivering out of shape to become splashes of green and brown and gold.

I pull the boat up the beach, put the fish in a bucket and walk up to the house. The weka know this routine. Two adults and four chicks appear running from under the house and take up position at the filleting table, eyes bright, ready for the offal. Shiny blue flies also come, and a slender-waisted yellow and black wasp. Everything seems to come together in celebration of sunlight, and I thank earth and sea for their abundance.

Somewhere between the births of Edward and Judith, I became concerned about the promise I'd made to Rosemary Callendar, my sixth-form English teacher. I don't know why this had become a responsibility but it worried me that I had done little creative writing since school. During the pharmacy years I wrote a story, sent it off to an English short story magazine and had it rejected; but study, exams and then babies had taken up time and energy. Life on the farm was busy, but it didn't demand intellectual energy. I decided to do something about that promise, and in 1958 I wrote a few stories in the evening, while the babies were asleep.

The stories were domestic, family themes, and the first was published in the *New Zealand Dairy Exporter*. That the editor David Yerex should write and ask for more work was a good sign. I was doing the right thing for my old teacher. There followed stories published in the *Home Journal*, School Publications, a story broadcast on the new radio programme *Country Calendar*; but my great desire was to sell a story to the *New Zealand Listener*. I thought if I could have a story published in the *Listener*, I would have fulfilled all writing ambition.

There were gaps in effort. When I was pregnant I was about as creative as a rice pudding, but in between I sent stories to *Listener* editor Monte Holcroft, who was in the habit of publishing a short story by some New Zealand writer every week. All my stories came back. The rejection slips were not bare, however; always there was some encouraging note, enough to make me try again. Eventually, came the note that made the difference. Mr Holcroft asked, 'How much rewriting do you do?'

Rewriting? What rewriting? I simply typed a story and sent it away. If I needed to rewrite it, what would I change? I didn't know. In the late 1950s there were no writing schools, no editing services. We had to find our own way.

Fortunately, about that time, I was invited to join a writers group that met in Palmerston North every second Friday night. Here, there were published women writers who were generous with their comments. They included Stanley Roche, Alice Glenday, Dell Adsett, Margaret Fuller, Wendy Simons. We formed a friendship based on trust, read manuscripts to each other, and offered each other the objective evaluation we lacked for our own work. I would advise any new writer to join a critique group. It is a rewarding experience in many ways, and writing skills grow rapidly.

In 1961, after more than forty rejections, I had a story published in the *Listener*. It may not have been the fulfilment of all ambition but it certainly was a peak experience. My feet were brought down to solid earth, though, by more rejection slips. But about six months later another story was accepted, and then another.

These were all stories recycled from experience, the familiar themes of family, marital disagreement and make-up, animals, gardens, moving house. An idea would rise out of memory, magnetically draw other ideas to it, and they would all coalesce in a story that wanted to become visible on paper.

But sooner or later, a writer will experience a story that comes not from the past but the future. I've discussed this with other writers and the only possible explanation we can find is that time is not linear but a spiral, and sometimes we encounter a future loop that has come close to us. Well, that sounds all right in theory, but how does it actually work?

Such a story of the future was 'The Silk', which was a powerful storm of thought that seemed to write itself in the early 1960s. It bore no resemblance to any part of my experience, apart from a childhood fascination with blue Willow Pattern china; yet its power has affected people as it affected me. That story has been filmed and reproduced in many anthologies, used in university courses, translated into other languages, and although I was frequently asked where I got the idea, I didn't know.

Then in 1985, my husband Malcolm and I lived the story of 'The Silk'. *When Mr Blackie took bad again that winter, he and Mrs Blackie knew it was for the last time . . .*

In June 1985, a month before he died, Malcolm reminded me that much of the story of 'The Silk' was being unwrapped for us from day to day. I had to agree. I'd become jealously possessive of him in the last weeks and importance was placed on small achievements such as buying and cooking food he could eat, and giving him his daily wash and massage to prevent bedsores. It was winter. The lawn was white with frost. I found fault with the visits from the district nurse. Yes, there were certain parallels.

Malcolm talked about the funeral. He said he wanted to wear the dressing gown I'd bought him as an engagement present.

Actually, he'd only had it on a couple of times – he always claimed it was 'too good' to wear around the house. I'd bought it in a men's outfitters in Palmerston North, after he'd proposed. It was different from the usual dressing gowns of wool or flannelette; it was an elegant robe of some kind of synthetic brocade in shades of blue, designed by Hardy Amies.

Malcolm died in the night while I was asleep beside him. My grief-filled response was, 'He didn't say goodbye!' It was what Mrs Blackie said about her husband, but at the time, I wasn't thinking of any fictitious character. The words were achingly mine.

Before the funeral director came, I took the Hardy Amies dressing gown out of the wardrobe, to iron it. I wondered about the temperature. Was it nylon? Polyester? I looked along the inside seams for information. There it was, a small blue label embroidered in black. The dressing gown was not synthetic. The label said, 100% pure silk.

In the early 1960s, on the strength of a handful of stories, Monte Holcroft nominated me for membership of PEN. I was dizzy with delight and anxiety – delight that somehow this meant I was a real author, and anxiety because people would know that I wasn't and consider me a fraud.

Soon after, I received an invitation to the PEN Christmas party at Wakefield House on The Terrace, took a deep breath and accepted. It meant a ride on the afternoon train from Palmerston North to Wellington, a short walk, a ride back on the evening limited express. I was nervous, but knew if I didn't go, I would regret the missed opportunity.

It was not difficult to find Wakefield House. I remember being impressed by the beautiful parquet floor (I was distressed, years later, to learn that it had disappeared under a property developer's bulldozer but that is another story.) I found myself in a large room full of people, cigarette smoke and noise. Most of the guests were at one end of the room. I stood in the middle of an empty space that seemed as big as Antarctica. I knew no one, and nobody saw me. The buzz of conversation was focused and busy, people waving hands to shape words and sloshing red wine in glasses.

I don't know how long I stood there – long enough to understand that I was a country girl who had invaded a sophisticated party under false pretences. I needed to go back and wait at the station until the evening train.

As I turned and walked towards the door, a woman who had been sitting in a chair near the wall stood up. She was tall, angular, wore a big brimmed hat and white gloves. She strode across the room towards me, held out a gloved hand and said in a loud, well-rounded voice, 'How do you do. The name is Marsh.'

I was rescued by a perceptive Ngaio Marsh, who escorted me to the other end of the room and introduced me to writers I knew by name only – Denis Glover, Noel Hilliard, Frank Sargeson, Ian Cross, Alistair Campbell. I discovered in the next hour that famous writers and poets were real people.

While short stories were being written for the *Listener* and radio, there was another strand of writing evolving from stories shared with the Cowley children. We lived in a house of invention, stories explaining the sound of the wind in the chimney, the squeak of a door, or the stuck drawer in the dressing table. The children joined in, embellishing tales and sometimes inventing them. Bath time tended to be game time, resulting in water on the floor, sodden towels and pyjamas, mushy soap and once, a number of toilet rolls unravelled in the toilet. The children invented a tiger that did all these things. But as the story grew so did the tiger, and the telling got out of control to the extent that four little Cowleys didn't want to go into the bathroom lest they were bitten by their tiger's sharp teeth.

It was time for me to enter the story. Placing a pair of pliers on a tray, I went into the bathroom, closed the door and proceeded to take out the tiger's teeth one by one, with all the appropriate yowling noises. The children were relieved. Now they could get back in the bath.

Later their tiger was recycled as a story in a *School Journal* about a tiger and a dental nurse, and in recent years, as a series character called Sloppy Tiger.

Story was everywhere, like fruit in our orchard. All I had to do was pick it up and use or preserve it for a later date.

Bedtime was official storytime. Each week we got books from the library but we also bought reject books, those well-loved library books with small rips and wrinkles, that sold for threepence or sixpence each.

Sharon, Judith and James loved fiction and could readily enter the world of a story. Not so our practical Edward who, at the age of five, had already earned the nickname of Mr Fixit. He chose library books about machinery, trains, tractors, trucks, how electricity worked. While I read E B White's *Charlotte's Web*, he played on the carpet with his Matchbox cars, saying, 'That's not true. Animals don't talk.'

Then I didn't know much about the wiring of the human brain and how children had different learning needs. I tried, with little success, to convert Edward to the books he rejected.

At this stage I was writing stories for School Publications, now known as Learning Media, with a special interest in easy-read stories for the *Part One Journal*. Learning Media has an established tradition of helping new writers, and I was one of their early apprentices, learning from Brian Birchall and Michael Keith the vocabulary requirements for the early levels, and the kind of stories they wanted to publish. I got nice letters from teachers and children about the *Journal* stories, but I had to admit they did not interest Edward. He was six and was not reading. His teacher at Whakarongo School, Gladys Thorley, suggested that I write stories for him about his interests. She took a copy of a Janet and John book from her table and said, 'There is no reason why children should want to read this.' She then gave me a Dolsch 100 basic word list, similar to the list I'd had from *School Journal* editor Brian Birchall, and I went home to begin little stories that would eventually dominate my writing for the rest of my life.

I soon realised that some words in the formal Dolsch word list were not common in child usage. They included *should, would, could* – almost never used by young children – whereas other well-used words such as *love* were omitted. I took a two-reel tape recorder to James'

Playcentre and recorded children's conversations. There was a lot of noise, of course, but the talk that came through made me aware of speech patterns and the words most frequently used.

In the 1980s, I learned that the Dolsch list had been made from adult business correspondence! I mentioned this at an International Reading Conference in America, and made a plea for a word list based on actual child usage. Some teachers assured me that this had been done and was in circulation.

I asked about the research.

One of them said, in all seriousness, 'The list was taken from children's books.'

Edward and the other children I worked with in the mid 1960s were my teachers, and the lessons I learned are still relevant today.

There was no point in presenting these children with the books they were supposed to be reading. They had met failure too many times and were not going to put themselves at risk again. Their body language was eloquent: elbows in at their sides, stiff posture, avoidance of eye contact. Many had been arbitrarily labelled dyslexic, and while I am sure that condition exists, I'm equally sure it did not affect any of these children. If I was being forced to learn Greek I would probably also write the letters back to front. No, these children had simply switched off to the mechanics of reading.

The way to reach them was through story.

We began a session with conversation and story talk. What did they do at the weekend? What pets did they have? What was their favourite food? Did they have a dream last night? If they could have three wishes, what would they be?

When they felt free to tell me their 'story', I typed it on my Olivetti portable with carbon paper included. Always it was recorded in the third person with the child's name appearing frequently in it, and in the title. The top copy was then given to the child to take home, and was read to him (all these children were boys) by parents, who reported that the child was eager to hear his own story. In the week before the next visit, I made a small, stapled book and put the story into simple language with some rough drawings so that the child could read it for himself. There were reading errors and hesitations, but never any reluctance. The child was the author of the book. He had 'authority'.

Edward's stories were mainly about life on the farm, and surprisingly, this boy who didn't like fiction was happy to have stories extended to fantasy in which he was the hero. 'Edward drives the hay baler. Edward saves the hay barn from burning down. Edward teaches his father to fly a topdressing plane.'

Once children were reading their own true stories, I could introduce them to new stories that included their names. I learned that it was important to empower them by making them heroes. Small was always the winner, and small solved any problem in a book. Children could come to the aid of adults, but not the other way around. I was working with young people who had experienced a certain amount of failure and they needed to have text that built up their self-esteem.

These children taught me the value of humour in a story. No one can be tense while they are laughing. I also developed a habit of putting a small surprise at the end of the book, which was a bit like pudding after vegetables, encouragement to read to the last page. I didn't know the habit had become so embedded until I was working in the garden with my seven-year-old granddaughter Lily. 'Don't walk through the rhubarb,' I told her. 'It is feeling fierce today and it might bite you on the ankles.'

Lily giggled. 'You want to make a story out of that, Granny, and put a twist at the end.'

Some of the stories written for Edward and other reluctant readers found their way into Palmerston North classrooms and were used by teachers who were making big books with brown paper, for group reading. There was a grassroots movement among reading teachers in those days, a resistance to dull expository text and an introduction of reading material that the children enjoyed. I knew teachers who made their own big books using popular nursery tales: *The Gingerbread Man, The Three Little Pigs, Goldilocks and the Three Bears, The Three Billy Goats Gruff.* But there was a limit to the amount of material available and new stories could not be used because of copyright issues. I wrote several very simple stories and plays for teacher friends to adapt for classroom use.

During this time, there were also stories for adults published in the *Listener*, a few of which were reprinted in an American magazine called *Short Story International*. One of these was 'The Silk', and it attracted the attention of a New York editor.

One day, an unfamiliar envelope with a Doubleday logo appeared in our rural delivery mailbox. A Doubleday editor, Anne Hutchens, had been passing through Grand Central Station on her way to work in Park Ave, when she picked up a copy of *Short Story International* and read the story. She liked it. Did I by any chance have a novel?

Blinded by opportunity, I promptly wrote back – no, I didn't have a novel but I was thinking about it.

Of course, I did think about it, rapidly, enthusiastically, and then hopelessly. I didn't know how to write a novel. The rush of brash confidence subsided and I went back to what I could do in the time left over from milking cows and looking after a family – little stories of a thousand words or less.

Six months later, there came another letter with the Doubleday logo. How was that novel coming along?

Miss Hutchens was still interested!

I sat down, wrote a long short story that might just be the first chapter of a novel, and sent it off. It was accepted. I received back a contract and promise of half the advance royalty.

That was the beginning of *Nest in a Falling Tree* and a lifelong friendship with Anne Hutchens.

Writing is a bit like night fishing. You go past the daylight of sensate experience into the warm dark interior where invisible stories wait for you. You don't know what they are, only that they are there. You bait your hook with an idea and lower it into the darkness.

Sometimes nothing happens and, disappointed, you row back to shore, the idea wilting on the hook. Other times, you feel the tug of a story then, suddenly, the bait is taken and the story is running with great energy. That's when you know what night fishing is all about.

At a children's writing workshop in Birmingham, Alabama, I was asked a profound question by a nine-year-old author. 'How do you know if an idea is a good one?'

I had to admit I didn't know, but added, 'If a story has a lot of energy and won't let me rest until it is written, I can be sure that it will have energy for the reader. On the other hand, if a story has poor energy, if I have to force it onto the paper, then it will probably be worthless.'

The young author nodded solemnly. He knew exactly what I meant.

The Early Novels

Nest in a Falling Tree was published by Doubleday NY in 1967, and by Secker & Warburg UK the following year. I'd borrowed the title from a line in a Tennessee Williams play: 'when a bird builds a nest . . . it doesn't build it in . . . a falling-down tree'; but when the German translation of the book came out, it was called *Ein Nest im Herbst Gebaut,* a nest in a tree in autumn – an interesting interpretation of 'falling'.

The book received good reviews in America and Britain, and because I'd never had a novel published before, I assumed that this was usual. But when the Secker & Warburg edition came to New Zealand, it was briefly reviewed, overlooked by bookstores and would have disappeared without a ripple had it not been for the attention of the English Faculty at Massey University, Palmerston North. An unexpected prelude to that attention came the year before when I received the advance copy of the American edition. It was beautiful – hand-cut pages of thick creamy paper and a rich blue cover bearing a quote that compared it with a Mozart sonata. A first novel, like a first baby, is infinitely precious and I did not want to let this one brand-new copy out of my hands. So I was very nervous when a Massey student doing an MA in English literature asked if he could borrow it. I made him promise that he would bring it back within two days. He read it promptly and returned it with a few kind remarks that seemed to me a little underwhelming. Then he added, 'They'll probably be doing it at Massey next year.'

With mock modesty, I said, 'I don't think that is likely.'

'Oh yes,' he said airily. 'They do anything up there.'

He was wrong. The English Faculty at Massey did not take the novel but they did adopt the author, so that thirty years later, the Hon Doc, Litt from Massey felt like a splendid homecoming.

Over the next decade I wrote another four novels for Doubleday: *Man of Straw*, *The Mandrake Root*, *Of Men and Angels* and *The Growing Season*, all set in New Zealand and all in our national literary genre, the bleak book. I believe it can be said that in New Zealand novels and films, the darkness is heavier than the light, and particularly in my own novels. The pages were so sodden with angst that they could be wrung out like handkerchiefs at a funeral. The later novels *Classical Music* and *Holy Days* were more balanced, but when I wrote them I had grown past the stage of therapy writing.

I have theories about the bleak book syndrome that other writers may not find acceptable. We all have within us a cave of pain where we have hidden our fears, hurts, resentments, beyond the daylight of conscious thought. But writing is a deep process, much like meditation. Monks have described the early stages of contemplative prayer as a dark time in which they were sorely tempted by evil thoughts. That's one way of looking at it. But the same process works for authors.

We can be sure that when we start writing, our pages will be like a Shakespearean play, littered with corpses. The trauma cave we no longer admit to having will be opened, and unresolved fear will be projected in our characters.

Of my own novels, I can only say that I am glad I did all my 'therapy writing' before I wrote novels for children. I see too many bleak manuscripts and books, especially in the young adult genre. Adolescence is a time of emotional extremes, but I don't think that a depressed teenager is going to feel better through a depressing book.

Once, at a Highlights Writing Workshop in Chautauqua, NY, I had a student who presented a very dark manuscript. When I suggested that life was a balance of light and shade, she told me that she did not feel very light-hearted. She said that three months before, her husband and children had died in a horrific accident. Her parents, well intended, had paid for her to go to the workshop, to help her 'get over' it.

I set her the task of writing about the accident and how she felt about it. She probably needed to write about it many times to ease the energy of her grief, and until she did that, she would not succeed with writing balanced stories for children.

For the rest of us who have a much smaller trauma cave, there is a place for therapy writing. It needs to be done, but in a journal.

So how do you know if your therapy writing is sneaking into a children's story? There is a sure sign. If you feel sorry for your character, that's it. We empathise with our characters, but we don't feel sympathy for them. If they make us a little tearful, then it is our own raw sadness that is being expressed.

I've found it easier to carry my problems than someone else's. After all, we can do something about our own lives, but we often feel helpless in the face of others' suffering.

Many of my generation felt this helplessness with the war in Vietnam. We tried the salve of anti-war demonstrations and took our guitars to coffee bars to sing protest songs made popular by Joan Baez or the Kingston Trio. What we were doing seemed comfortable, even romantic, compared with the reality of the Vietnam invasion.

I encountered that reality not so much through sanitised news, but through letters from my young cousin Soren Gedge, who was serving his second term there in the army. He wrote of atrocities that I thought were in his imagination. When I discovered they were true, I wanted to tear down the sky in a great howl of rage.

About the same time, Price Milburn advertised a competition for a children's picture book story. Suddenly I had an idea, wheels to take the anti-war energy somewhere productive. This message needed to go to the next generation, and anger was not the right vehicle for it.

I remembered an account I'd read about a duck that had laid her eggs on a building site somewhere in the United States, and how work was stopped for three weeks until the eggs were hatched. I entered the picture book competition with a story called 'The Duck in the Gun'.

It won the competition, but after a year Price Milburn decided they could not publish it, and they returned the rights to me. I sent the story to my Doubleday friend Anne Hutchens, who passed it on to their children's editor. It was published in 1969, with illustrations by graphic artist Edward Sorel, better known for his satirical cartoons in *Playboy* magazine. When the book went out of print, it came back to New Zealand and was published in 1983 by Wendy Pye, with beautiful illustrations from Robyn Belton. This is the edition that was taken by the Hiroshima Peace Memorial Museum.

The Duck in the Gun was published again in 2008 by Walker Books, and is still in print.

The message goes on, and although there is no way to calculate its effect, for me, the story was peace-making, turning my protest anger into something less ugly. But then story always does that. It has the habit of bringing us home to ourselves.

In 1968 there were two offers of film rights for the first novel, *Nest in a Falling Tree*. I favoured the enquiry from Geraldine Page's agent, simply because I admired Geraldine Page's acting ability. The other offer came from Roald Dahl, who wanted to make a film for his wife Pat Neal, who was then recovering from a series of strokes. Doubleday made the choice and accepted Roald Dahl's offer on my behalf, probably because Roald was ready to pay quite a lot of money.

August 1970, when the film was being made, Malcolm and I were invited to visit the Dahls. We took a train from London to Buckinghamshire, got off at the station feeling a little self-conscious, and were relieved to see an ordinary-looking man leaning against an ordinary-looking car. He chatted amiably about the film as he drove us to Gipsy House, where we met Pat. 'I won't remember your names,' she said in that famous husky voice. 'But I do remember faces.'

Malcolm and I were impressed by Roald's glittering intelligence and Pat's warmth. We sat outside over pre-dinner drinks, watching masses of budgerigars flying into the orchard, as bright as jellybeans in the low sunlight.

'When I had my stroke, I wanted a budgie,' Pat explained. 'Roald bought me two hundred. They've now multiplied.'

They showed us the swimming pool Roald had designed, with a domed roof and solar heating – Roald's invention before it was known elsewhere. They also invited us to try a waterbed – also Roald's invention, and not heated. We had heaps of feather quilts to keep out the cool evening air.

Over dinner they talked more about the film and Roald's latest book. He said he'd finished with short stories and had written a children's novel called *Charlie and the Chocolate Factory*, which was with the publisher.

I don't remember the rest of the conversation or what we ate for dinner. In 1970 I was still quite ignorant of alcohol and I had drunk martinis as though they were lemonade. I happily agreed to an after-dinner swim in the beautiful blue pool, but almost as soon as I dived in, I polluted it by throwing up. The others got out quite quickly and I stood there, suddenly shocked sober, unable to say anything except, 'Sorry, sorry –'

They were warmly gracious, and Pat told me the story of her Oscar. She had received an Academy Award for her role in *The Subject Was Roses*, but at the time she was in England, recovering from the strokes. Audrey Hepburn accepted the award on Pat's behalf, and when Pat was well enough to travel, she and Roald went to the States to meet Audrey Hepburn in a New York restaurant. They had lunch together and Pat, being nervous, drank too much wine. She said she did what I had done, but over Audrey Hepburn. I did wonder if the story had been invented to make me feel better; but then Roald reinforced the tale and brought out a heavy gold statue that they tossed around as though it had been won in a sideshow.

We kept in touch for several years, although the last letters from Roald were rather sad: ill health, another failed hip surgery, failed marriage. As for the film of *Nest in a Falling Tree*, it was released as *The Road Digger*; the quiet love story was given the Dahl touch to become a macabre thriller about a young man who was a necrophiliac and had to murder the women with whom he fell in love.

I didn't mind. They could have made it into a musical for all I cared. The money they paid for the film rights bought Fish Bay.

Roald Dahl once sent me a photo of himself and Pat in the jerseys I had spun and knitted for them. They never did see the bay, but they were pleased that we'd acquired it with the film money; and the woollen garments meant another connection.

Until a few years ago, we kept a few sheep in the bay – a flock of Romney/Perendale cross, looked after by Hans and Maree Gerritsen of Waitaria Bay – and each year I would keep one or two of the best fleeces for spinning.

These days, I tend to recognise the vegetation in the bay by its capacity to yield dye: kanuka bark – pinkish fawn; foxgloves – jade green; gum leaves – gold; silver dollar gum – orange; *Sticta coronata* lichen – shades of mauve and purple; elderberries – red; five-finger berries – grey; flax flowers – dark brownish-red; and so on. The vegetation is gathered in season and stored in the freezer until I am ready to use it.

'Be careful what you get out of Mum's freezer,' my children used to warn their friends. 'You could poison yourself.'

That is not the only comment they offer. When people have commented on the vegetable dyes in Fairisle jerseys, the young Cowleys have been quick to say, 'Ask Mum how she gets the blue colour.'

This has happened so often that I might as well reveal the secret here, and you people who spin and knit can decide what to do with it.

Blue comes from indigo but everyone knows that it is impossible to get a colourfast indigo dye. There is an elaborate process using fixing agents that helps, but fading is inevitable. Even if we don't dye wool, we know how indigo fades in denim clothing.

Dye books tell us that Native American peoples used to make indigo colourfast in their weavings, but the formula has been lost.

I mentioned this to a Hopi weaver living in Southern California. She laughed. 'It's not lost. Our indigo-dyed wool never fades. Those people just don't like the way we do it, so we don't tell them.'

So, do you want to know? You need half a plastic bucket of a woman's urine. Don't ask me why it has to be from a woman. This is what I was told. With a stick, stir in your indigo powder. It will not mix but will lie on the top of the urine. Now put the bucket away in some dark warm place, preferably a shed far from the house. Stir every day. Over a few days, the urine will ferment and as it ferments the indigo will dissolve. When all the powder has dissolved, put in skeins of wool pre-washed in warm water and detergent to remove all grease. Keep stirring every day. After a week, you will get a teal blue colour. After two weeks the wool will be deep blue. Put on rubber gloves, remove wool from bucket and wash thoroughly – several times.

The colour will not fade.

Once I had a bucket 'maturing' under the house. An electrician arrived to fix a hot point and said he had to find a cable under the house. I cringed but said nothing. He came out, wrinkling his nose. 'You need to get something done about your septic tank!' he exclaimed. 'It's terrible!'

I still didn't tell him.

My lovely children did.

The sheep have now gone from the bay and bush is reclaiming all but small areas kept for gardens around the houses. But I still get wool from neighbours in the Sounds, still treadle the spinning wheel in the evenings. I don't eat meat, but I get much pleasure from preparing and wearing sheep's wool clothing.

The years with Doubleday, 1966–78, established friendships that are still strong. My editor Anne needed to work for another publisher when she married Doubleday's editor-in-chief, Ken McCormick, and I was passed on to Lisa Drew.

Editor/author relationships are special; I know of no connections like them in the rest of the commercial world. Books and lives are shared through correspondence, and for me, the exchanges span a length of history, airmail letters and long-distance cable calls with their ghost-like echoes, faxes curling slowly from a machine, and now the shuttle-speed of emails. Several of my American editors have come to New Zealand: Anne McCormick, of course, Lisa Drew, Patti Gauch of Philomel, Adria Klein from Dominie, people from The Wright Group in Washington State.

Lisa Drew, who eventually went to William Morrow and built her own imprint, came to New Zealand in 1976 and Edward and I drove her around the North and South islands during her three-week stay.

Lisa came from a family who had great respect for the American flag, and with this awareness, it was important to Lisa that she see a New Zealand flag. But in 1976, New Zealanders were not at all flag conscious. There were empty flagpoles everywhere and no souvenir flags available in shops. I promised Lisa that in Wellington, she would see our flag flying outside Parliament. But no, there was none there either, because Parliament wasn't in session. On the second-to-last day of her visit, we eventually found a New Zealand flag. Where? Outside the American embassy!

For years, Lisa had been working with Alex Haley on his epic book *Roots*. The final manuscript was supposed to have come to Doubleday before she left on vacation, but it hadn't, and she doubted if it would be on her desk when she got back. But it did arrive during her absence. Lisa's colleague Sally Arteseros sent a telegram with the glad news.

This telegram got an odd reception at our local post office. I answered the phone and a somewhat frosty voice announced that there was a cablegram for Miss Lisa Drew care of our address.

'She's out at the moment,' I said. 'Please, can you read it out and I'll write it down for her.'

The voice got even colder. 'No! The message cannot be read out over the phone. Please, tell her to come to the post office to collect it.'

Poor Lisa! She was bewildered by an indifferent reception at the post office counter and came back commenting on the rudeness of the staff. I looked at the cablegram, interpreting it in the context of Kiwi word usage. Obviously, the women in the Post Office had considered 'roots in at last love sally' to be indecent.

A few days later a florist delivered a huge bouquet of red roses, a gift to Lisa from a grateful Alex Haley.

During those years, I also visited New York – four times, I think.

Each visit, I called in at the Doubleday offices in the Chemical Bank Building in Park Ave. On the last visit, I could not find my editor. The room was occupied by a woman I knew, but her name escaped me. The woman was small, slender, black straight hair, black sweater and pants, no make-up. She greeted me warmly. Yes, I was expected, would I please follow her and she'd take me, and wasn't it difficult trying to find the way around these buildings? While she chatted, I rebuked myself for forgetting her name. Not for long. We almost collided with someone I did know well, who greeted me, then said, 'I see you've met Jackie.'

The woman was Jackie Onassis. I had not met her before, but of course her face was familiar. She was working as an editor at Doubleday, and a very good editor too. Before I left she gave me an autographed copy of a book of Russian fairytales she had edited (and if the person who later borrowed it is reading this, I would dearly love to have it back).

Visits to New York always included catch-up time with Anne McCormick. One night in 1970, Anne and her nine-month-old son

John entertained me at supper. Over a cheese soufflé we talked books, babies and friendship, and I promised Anne that I would dedicate a book to John.

That book would be *The Silent One*.

The story of *The Silent One* began in 1971 with time in Fiji. First experiences usually make a strong impression, and there were many firsts that visit – first tropical island, first coconut palms, first time snorkelling over a reef, first experiences of Fijian culture and art. I was on sensate overload.

Before we left New Zealand, a teacher at the School for the Deaf in Whanganui had asked me if I could write something for and about deaf children. I thought that perhaps I could, because my father, who had recently died, had been profoundly deaf. But the request was forgotten in the excitement of the Fiji visit.

Malcolm was auditor for two tourist resort projects, and while he was away working, I wandered around Suva, absorbing all that newness. One morning, in the fish market, I saw something that cut me to the heart. Lying upside down on the concrete floor was a large turtle, feebly waving its flippers, water streaming from eyes that were full of stress. I knew that if I didn't do something, it would be killed and eaten. But I had no money, no way of getting it back to the sea. I had to wait until Malcolm came back to our hotel. I would ask him to buy it, then maybe we could get it into a taxi and take it to the harbour.

As I hoped, Malcolm returned before the market closed and he did not dispute my plan. We would buy the turtle and release it. We hurried down to the wet section of the market.

The turtle had gone. It had been sold mid-afternoon and was probably already dead.

We were both quiet over dinner that night, but often an inner quiet is the beginning of story. A rhythm of words begins to vibrate in the silence, and then ideas coalesce, bonding, changing shape, taking on new life – threatened turtle, deaf child, the silent world of the reef.

I didn't have the Olivetti portable in Fiji, so I bought a bunch of exercise books and some pens. The first draft of *The Silent One* was finished before it was time to go back to Wellington.

It took much longer to find a publisher. I sent the manuscript out to five publishers in New Zealand and overseas, and received cautious praise with rejection. They all said much the same thing. It was well written but it was neither an adult book nor a children's book and would have no market.

In 1978, when I was fully involved in writing early reading material, Max Rogers of Whitcoulls Publishing suggested that I try a children's novel.

I replied, 'I did one once. It was a flop.'

'Have you still got it?' he asked. 'Let me see it.'

I pulled the manuscript out of storage and sent it to him, expecting a response similar to those I'd had. But obviously, in seven years, literary fashion had changed. Max sent back a telegram. 'It is marvellous and it must be published.'

Whitcoulls then launched an art competition for a suitable illustrator and I was invited to Christchurch to look at the shortlist. The clear winner was Sherryl Jordan – and there began another valued friendship. While she was working on *The Silent One*, Sherryl said that she loved drawing and painting, but what she really wanted to do was write books. Her decision to do something about her longing was the beginning of a career as author of a long list of fine books, all written with an artist's eye.

The Silent One sold in the South Pacific and was awarded Children's Book of the Year 1982 in the inaugural Government Printer Awards, now the New Zealand Post Book Awards.

It was my first children's novel and I wanted it to be dedicated to John McCormick, who was now nine years old, but I knew that it would not be sold in America from New Zealand. I sent a copy to Anne McCormick at Knopf, who passed it on to the children's book department, Pantheon, and it was accepted. They published a fine American edition with engravings by Hermann Greissle and a back-cover photo of me and John, taken by Ken McCormick.

At last, John had his book. Now I sit here hoping for inspiration for a book I can dedicate to John's seven-year-old daughter Natalie, Anne's treasured grandchild.

The story of *The Silent One* didn't finish in New York. It went on to be published in twelve languages, mainly due to the influence of the film made by the Gibson Group from a script written by Ian Mune.

Dave Gibson and Yvonne Mackay chose to shoot the film in Aitutaki in the northern Cook Islands group. It was an ambitious undertaking full of challenge: a white turtle, a shark attack, a hurricane, an entire film crew with all its gear moving onto a quiet island. It is a tribute to Dave and Yvonne that they managed it, and only because they, and everyone involved, had masses of Kiwi ingenuity and resilience. There was no electricity to power wind machines, so they took to the island a DC3 aircraft, minus its wings, so the props could create wind for the hurricane. Monsoon buckets on a tipping apparatus provided the flood water.

While the film was being made, Edward and I stayed in the resort hotel on Aitutaki, next door to Pat Evison, who played Luisa. Zac Wallace, who had recently completed the film *Utu*, was there in the part of Tasiri; and singer-entertainer Prince Tui Teka was in the role of the post office/store keeper. Prince Tui Teka's role may have been small in the film, but on the island his generosity was in keeping with his stature. He did a free concert for locals, who still remember him with awe and gratitude.

Australian shark experts Ron and Valerie Taylor did the underwater filming. It was Val who supervised the catching of a large tiger shark and its introduction to the enclosed lagoon where most of the filming took place. This shark had been caught on a large hook on piano wire. Val, who treated sharks like pet dogs, had carefully plugged the hole near the shark's mouth with cotton wool and a healing ointment.

The afternoon we arrived, Val offered me fins, mask and snorkel. 'Come in and see it,' she said, meaning the man-eating shark. 'It's beautiful.'

I politely declined but she insisted, saying that she and Ron would swim on either side of me.

That's all very well, I thought, but they are skinny and I am not. If that shark is hungry it won't even look at them.

However, I did go in, which just goes to show that some of us would rather die than make fools of ourselves. I swam slowly around the lagoon, and I don't know which was worse, seeing the shark, or not seeing it.

I didn't stay in long. While Val was trying to show me up close how she had plugged the hole made by the hook, I started striking out for the shore.

I felt much sympathy for sixteen-year-old Aucklander Telo, who played Jonasi. He had a whole day of shooting with the shark, and he was terrified.

Without doubt, Aitutaki was a good choice for the set. The sunlight was bright, unpolluted, and its effect through blue water was dramatic. I've watched the film many times for its visual impact and also for Jenny McLeod's music, which is stunningly beautiful.

Family Matters

My children look for themselves in my writing and are quick to pick up on any family stories I may have used. I told them I would not use their stories in this book but I must stretch that promise a little, for they are such a large part of my life that, without them, I would be a very different person. My children too have been my teachers, and that is ongoing.

Sharon, Judith and James lived in Wellington. Edward stayed in Palmerston North to do an aircraft mechanical engineering apprenticeship with Field Air. For a while he lived at the farmhouse with Ted and his wife Jennie, then he moved to a little cottage on the farm. Growing up, all four spent their holidays in Fish Bay.

The summer we read *Lord of the Rings*, the girls renamed the area. Linkwater became The Shire; features of the road into the bay were named for the Hobbit's journey; the neighbour's horse became Shadowfax; and Sharon's cat was Took because he was 'more Took than Baggins'.

Edward and James used to sail around the bay in an old P Class that had belonged to their stepbrother Andrew Mason. It had lost mast, rudder and sails, but that was easily fixed. A manuka pole for the mast, some wood from a fruitbox for a rudder and they were off. When I saw their green and white sail in the bay, I understood what had happened to the missing double-bed sheet.

At Queen Margaret, Sharon did well at art and when her own family was growing up, she completed an MA in Fine Arts at Auckland University of Technology. She now has her own studio and paints full-time. When she left school she went nursing, training at Wellington Hospital, a career well suited to her caring, compassionate disposition.

Judith too, is a natural healer. She did science subjects at university but since then her journey has taken her to employment where she functions as massage therapist, mentor, teacher and rehabilitator. She paints delicate watercolours and has done some book illustration. Her paintings in a simple reading text called *Dinner* are greatly loved by children in the United States, and I warm with pleasure when their letters arrive with the question, 'Is Judith Cowley related to you?'

James borrows from both sides of the family – he is visually creative like his sisters but has also the hands-on practical inventiveness of his father and brother. He left school to enter the film world, working for his uncle Graeme Cowley and now, more than thirty years later, is a director of cinema-photography.

It was James who coined the term Club Fed for the tribal summers we spend in the bay. We are all passionate about food, and the long evening meals in the courtyard are a tradition that prompted Janice, Edward's wife, to publish the Fish Bay culinary history in a cookbook.

This preoccupation with food goes back a long way. When James was ten and Sharon was fourteen, I suggested that the children might like to keep a diary of their summer holiday adventures. James's effort was brief. He wrote on the wall calendar under each date. 'Mum made bread. Mum made bread. Mum made bread. Mum didn't make bread.'

When I was very young, five or six, my Scottish grandmother told me I had the 'shine'. I didn't know what she meant and still don't know but can circumnavigate the word with guesses. Grandma said she had it and her mother before her.

'There's but the ain in every family wha' has it handed doon,' she said.

My best guess is that she meant some kind of intuitive knowing that comes without warning. If so, she is wrong about there being only one in each family. Both Sharon and Judith also have it.

One night, Sharon, Judith and I all had a dream with slight variations but the same result. In these dreams, Edward, who was doing parachute jumping, fell to the earth and was killed. We were so shaken by this, that we nagged at Edward until I think he half-believed us. He gave away the parachute jumps to take up hang-gliding. He was good at it and became a hang-gliding instructor in Palmerston North.

One Sunday in early August 1979, not long after his 21st birthday, Edward's hang-glider ripped at 600 ft and he fell to the earth.

That day, there was a Spanish day for extension students at Victoria University. We'd had films, talks, debates *en español* and then a break for *tapas* and *sangria*. Everyone was in celebratory mood, but a few minutes before 4.00 pm I became ill, seized with a cold so deep it seemed like hypothermia. I excused myself and left; I was scarcely able to drive, so severe was the shivering.

Sharon, who had just come off her nursing duty, ran a hot bath for me but that made no difference. My teeth were chattering. My bones seemed set in ice. Malcolm was wondering if he should call the family doctor, when the phone rang. A young man, one of Edward's friends, was calling from Palmerston North. In a strained voice, he told us that there had been a hang-gliding accident on a farm at Tokomaru.

Edward was in hospital and we should go there as soon as possible.

The accident had happened at 3.55 pm.

Edward was in a cot in the intensive care unit, in a deep coma, severely brain-damaged, bleeding from the ears and nose. One arm was fractured. He'd landed on his knees, so both legs had fractures and one had been driven up through his pelvis. The hospital staff had shaved his head but his condition was too fragile for surgery to relieve pressure on his brain. The doctor told us there was a chance he'd make it through the night, but his eyes said otherwise.

My shivering had stopped but I barely noticed that. I sat in a chair by the bed, feeling that I was wrestling with something much more powerful than myself.

During the night, the heartbeat on the monitor scribbled like a seismograph, very rapid, and then fell away to a flat line; I put my hands on Edward and saw the heartbeat pick up again. Time and time again, it happened. Each time the alarm went off, the night staff looked up and once a nurse said gently, 'Don't build up your hopes too much.'

He was still alive in the morning, but in the same precarious condition. His pulse staggered. I put my hands on him, talked to him; his heartbeat steadied.

Ted and his wife Jennie were travelling in England and we had no contact details for them. The other children were devastated by Edward's accident and found it difficult to hold in their emotion. But Sharon had a nursing friend, Tracey Carter, who stepped into the gap. Tracey simply left work and sat with me by the bed, taking over when I needed sleep.

Palmerston North Hospital staff allowed me to stay by Edward for the six weeks he was in hospital. Recovery was slow. A doctor showed me X-rays and said I'd need to think about Edward's future. He'd had, in effect, a massive stroke, wiping out his speech motor centre. He wouldn't talk again.

We accepted the gloomy news. No matter what the outcome, Edward was ours and we would look after him.

Three weeks after the accident, and no longer in intensive care, Edward lay in a small room surrounded by family. He was still unconscious, though frowning deeply and grunting from time to time.

Suddenly, he interrupted our conversation. 'Will you please pull the curtains,' he said. 'The light's hurting my eyes.'

We all cried. The doctor had been wrong.

It was another two weeks before he spoke again, but he steadily improved and at the end of six weeks left hospital to go home in my care. I stayed with him at his cottage for another two weeks and when Ted and Jennie came back to New Zealand in October, Edward was able to meet them at Wellington airport.

Today there is no evidence of the brain damage except a slight droop at the corner of his mouth when he is tired.

Since Edward's accident, I've known other families who have had a child in a similar situation. My plea has been, 'Stay beside the bed! Don't leave him! Keep your hands on him!'

I tell Edward's story now to reinforce this message. In the Western world we know so little about the energy fields of the human body and the way we can pass energy on to someone who needs it.

A Ramakrishna swami told me that the palms of the hands are energy centres. He said that when young monks begin meditation, their hands get very hot and they are instructed to place their hands on the sick and the old – people who need that energy. If they don't, he said, the skin on the hands breaks down and their palms start to bleed.

I immediately thought of the Western tradition, where monks do not touch anyone.

I believe that sometime in the future, a study of human energy fields and auras will become a part of our medical research. I also believe that a baby's stem cells, retained in the mother, let the mother know when something happens to her child – which may account for maternal instinct. It might also explain what I felt at the moment of Edward's accident.

There is not much scientific evidence as yet, but in the meantime, we should trust our instincts and give of our energy when it is needed.

Early Reading Books

The window in front of me frames a view of soft rain falling on the green umbrellas of tree ferns, mist draped across the shoulders of the hills, a flat incoming tide in shades of green and charcoal grey.

Once, on a day such as this, I described the scene in a reply to some year three children who had sent me a letter. I wrote: *This is a good day for fishing. Soon I'll go out in my little boat, and I hope the fish are biting.*

About a week later, the class teacher sent back a response from a seven-year-old boy. He had drawn an elaborate dinghy with portholes and an anchor, and a figure in the bow with a line over the side. Above the picture he had written: *I like fishing but I don't like to get bitted.*

I wish it had been possible to keep the children's letters and art work I've received over the past forty years. Some favourites have been saved and these fill stacks of cardboard cartons in a storeroom. They include a letter from a nine-year-old Californian girl doing an author project. Her questions were usual: *How many children do you have? What are the names of your pets? What is your favourite food?* – but the last question had me thinking: *Are you still alive?*

There is the letter from the six-year-old girl who told me, *I have two pets a dog and a turtle. The turtle lays eggs. The dog does not lay eggs.* And a business proposition from an eight-year-old entrepreneur – *Do you want good ideas for your stories? I have lots of good ideas. They won't cost you very much.*

Every letter tells me something about the writer, and something about myself. Always, these letters remind me why I so enjoy writing for children. How many adult friends draw butterflies and dinosaurs on envelopes or tape a lollipop onto a letter?

I can't remember who said, 'When I grow up I want to be a child', but I echo that wish. It is very likely that it will be granted.

In 1978, New Zealand teachers were actively campaigning for new early reading books that had the same high standard of text and illustration as the *School Journals* and international picture books. For decades, writers such as myself had been fostered by *School Journal* editors, so that the School Publications offices in the old wooden Government Buildings were hothouses of child-centred creativity for New Zealand writing and art.

But for some reason the same high standard didn't include the books that children encountered when they started school. Perhaps, as a new nation, we were not confident in our ability to produce good early reading material, believing that England and America did it better.

My parents' generation had the English Beacon Readers; I failed the phonics-based Whitcombe & Tombs Progressive Primers, also English; and my children had the Janet and John version of the American basal Dick and Jane books. The New Zealand Education Department's Ready-to-Read books were introduced later, and were a great improvement. New Zealand children were reading about themselves in situations that they recognised. But the initial programme was tentative, experimental and small in scope. Almost immediately it was obvious that Ready-to-Read needed to be expanded and upgraded.

Price Milburn produced a good supplementary series modelled on Ready-to-Read vocabulary, and this sold well. However, these too were small books, economically produced, and children did not see their school readers as 'real books'. There was a huge gap in quality between the fine trade picture books being published overseas and the official reading books children were given when they started school.

I asked a publisher, 'Why can't early reading books have the same quality as commercial picture books?'

The publisher replied that reading texts needed to be sold cheaply to schools, and no publisher could afford to produce them at that standard.

I argued, 'But a commercial picture book has a short life. An educational book has many reprints and an average life of ten years. Wouldn't the ongoing sales warrant the expense?'

The publisher said, no, it would not. To produce reading texts of the quality of glossy picture books would be commercial suicide.

School Publications were less pessimistic. The publication arm of the Department of Education had formed a new branch, Learning Media, to address the upgrade of Ready-to-Read. The aim was to bridge the gap with reading texts that looked like 'real books'. In 1978, they gathered a group of *School Journal* authors and illustrators together at Tatum Park, Waikanae, and we spent a weekend bouncing ideas off each other.

I took with me some stories I had written for teacher friends, and also wrote a few new tales, some of which were accepted.

That was the weekend that Greedy Cat was born.

When we lived in Everest Street, Khandallah, children would some-times call at the house after school – with parental permission, of course. We'd have chocolate milk and a biscuit and discuss current interests. One young lady said her family had a new cat.

'What's it called?' I asked.

She thought for a moment, then said, 'Well, it's got a real name but it's greedy so we just call it Greedy Cat.'

I did what all authors do, plucked the jewel out of the air and stored it in the resource library of memory. Later, the title would fit a dear old rascal visualised by Robyn Belton.

Robyn had done a marvellous illustration for my *School Journal* story, 'My Tiger' but we didn't meet until that weekend at Tatum Park. She had her pencils and watercolours and I had a story about a cat thief:

> He looked in the shopping bag,
> gobble, gobble, gobble,
> and that was the end of that.

The story was accepted and Learning Media put Robyn and me together to work out the illustrations. What a splendid time we had! It doesn't take much for either of us to drop the adult façade, and when we work together on a story, we enter it as two children, exploring a range of delicious jokes and puns, literally and visually. Although we must have had some serious discussions about images and layout,

I can't remember anything much except laughter. There was one design change, I recall. Greedy Cat was originally grey. I knew from experience that black or grey printed in an illustration, tended to look like a hole in the paper. So the old rascal became a ginger cat.

Robyn's daughter Katie was a toddler at the time. She went into the book, as did Robyn's old bicycle and furniture from her house in Nelson.

Katie is now about the same age we were when Greedy Cat was created, and Robyn and Peter Belton now live in Dunedin.

Greedy Cat is also getting long in the whiskers, but his appetite for food and ways to get it is still unbounded. He occasionally breaks the format of books to send emails to Robyn, and he yowls in triumph when he gets quacking replies from the duck in the gun.

The Tatum Park experiment yielded a bunch of promising manuscripts for the new Ready-to-Read extensions, but the stories had to be evaluated by teachers, and Learning Media, in true democratic spirit, decided that they should go to all early reading teachers in New Zealand. This system was admirable in theory but unwieldy, and it was later amended. It greatly postponed publication dates that were urgent even before Tatum Park. We learned that the first of these new books would not be available until 1983. That was five years away!

I looked at a bunch of stories I had – some new, others that had been well used by teachers – and thought about the publication of a small batch of about twenty beautifully illustrated 'real' books for children, that would help fill the gap until the new Ready-to-Read books came out. I knew that no existing publisher would be prepared to put quality production into reading texts, but I talked it over with Malcolm, who believed in the idea and was prepared to fund it.

There was another concern. I could not do this project on my own. I needed to work with someone with background knowledge of the teaching of reading. June Melser was the obvious candidate.

June had been a classroom teacher and a Teachers College lecturer. She'd also worked for School Publications and had been the interim editor of the Ready-to-Read extensions until Margaret Mooney was appointed. Although June was passionate about children having good books, she declined and I didn't know why. But then, a few weeks later, she phoned me and I realised she'd been diffident because she was committed to a publisher. Yes, she would do it, she said, but on one condition: would I be prepared to show my manuscripts to Wendy Pye?

Who was Wendy Pye?

'She's a new publisher in Auckland,' June said. 'She's got my collection of retold folk tales. I think she's the right person to do this. Why don't you go to Auckland and meet her?'

That's how I met Wendy Pye, the publisher at Shortland Publications, a division of New Zealand News – and I was impressed. She was young, had strong energy, sharp intelligence, cutting honesty and a wealth of enthusiasm. I knew instantly that she was the right person.

June had sent Wendy copies of my stories and Wendy had passed them on to early reading experts in Auckland for evaluation. She'd got positive feedback and was ready to start on the first batch of sixteen books.

At this stage, Wendy's in-house staff consisted of her secretary Sandy Clark and Bruce Wallace, art director. There were some part-time editors and consultants, but nearly all the work was done by Wendy and her small team. This was to our advantage. In big publishing houses, books tend to be processed on an assembly line, which is not the best way to produce early reading material. Ours were done around a table.

June came up with the name Story Box, and she added some more retold folk tales to the scripts. We arranged with Wendy that the illustrators would receive a royalty for their work – something that hadn't been done by other publishers of early reading books. We thought that would attract illustrators, but actually most of the people we approached were 'too busy' and some didn't reply to the letters of enquiry. Who could blame them? Picture books of eight and sixteen pages? No advance, just a royalty? It must have sounded all rather dodgy.

I contacted polytechs, art schools and advertising agencies and found young artists, some of them students, who were interested in illustrating children's books. Wendy, Bruce, June and I went through samples of their work. Most of it was very good but too sophisticated or adult for young children, but we did find some excellent child-friendly illustrators in Elizabeth Fuller, Philip Webb, Rodney McRae, Jenni Webb, as well as established children's illustrators Robyn Belton and Dick Frizzell.

I've already mentioned the special relationship that can exist between authors and their editors. The Story Box connection was wider than that. There were four of us, June, Wendy, Bruce, me, and we met at each other's houses, illustrations spread across table and floor, as we shifted a word here, a word there, fine-tuning the production. June and I saw every stage of the book from the child view, and Wendy and Bruce trusted us in that. Illustrations provided reading clues and could have nothing more or less than was in the text. Characters in illustrations had to be introduced in the same order that they were in the text. The movement in the art had to be from left to right to help appropriate page-turning. The line breaks were breathing pauses that had to retain meaning. We needed fonts that had the right letter shapes for new readers. Text had to have exactly the right position on the page.

When the first sixteen Story Box Read-Together books came

out, June and I were bewildered by their reception. They sold out immediately and teachers wanted more. Our plan to produce a few books as a Band-Aid to cover a gap became something bigger, and now Wendy was looking at the possibility of a full reading programme.

To those teachers who wondered at the structure of Story Box, seemingly made up of 'bits and pieces', this is the explanation. It simply kept growing in demand.

If this surprised June and me, we were even more amazed at Wendy's entrepreneurial ability. She sold Story Box in Australia and England, then filled suitcases with books and went to the Bologna Book Fair. There she met Tom and Arlene Wright, who had been selling educational material out of their garage in San Diego and who wanted an early reading programme. Tom often told the story of selling Arlene's car for the airfare to the Bologna Book Fair and there meeting this tall, friendly, Down-Under publisher who assured them she had the best thing since sliced bread.

Story Box went to the United States in 1981 and is still being published there.

Sometimes June Melser and I worked at her house near Masterton, and sometimes at the house in the Sounds.

It was a winter morning in the bay and I had been out fishing. June was sitting at the table by the fire, surrounded with paper, pencils, erasers, notes.

'I'm freezing,' I told her, as I put some flounder in the sink. 'I'm going to have a hot bath before breakfast.'

I filled up the old tub with eagle's feet, added bath essence and lay back in bliss, staring dreamily at the match-lining walls and swishing a face flannel through the water. Wishy-washy, wishy-washy.

The watery words opened a door in my mind and some characters rushed in: four animals, a bustling woman farmer who was neurotic about cleanliness, and a tin tub. *'O lovely mud,' said the cow and she jumped in it.* I sat up in the bath, alert with story. *Along came Mrs Wishy-Washy. 'Just look at you!' she screamed.*

I was out of the bath, dried and dressed in no time, and running out to the kitchen. 'June! June! I've got another story!'

June already had the pencil in her hand. I dictated. She wrote. At the end she counted the paragraphs and said, 'Too long! One of the animals has to go.'

'Okay,' I said, 'cut out the dog.'

Years later, there was a book called *Wishy-Washy Day* with the dog in it. Children asked me, 'When did Mrs Wishy-Washy get a dog?'

'He's always been there,' I replied. 'But we had to take him out of the first book because there was no room for him.'

Another question I am often asked is, 'Where did you get the idea for Mrs Wishy-Washy?'

I used to say I didn't know, that she simply jumped into my head from nowhere, while I was in the bath.

But of course, ideas never come from nowhere. I had to go a long way back to find the source of that story, but there it was – Mother, Father, three little girls, living in an old house without electricity. Every morning and night we had cold washes, although sometimes the water was warmed from the kettle on the wood stove.

Once a week, a wishy-washy type of tin tub was brought in and put in front of the fire. The old copper in the washhouse was lit, water heated, and then our parents would bucket in hot water to fill the tin tub. Three little girls would be sent outside while Mum and then Dad had the first baths. Then Joan, Heather and I would be called in. We all got in the tub together, as slippery as eels. I remember the pleasure of it, the hot water, the splashing, the warm towels on the rack above the stove. At some stage, though, our mother came in with a bar of yellow soap in one hand and a washcloth in the other, and that's when the fun dropped dead. Children who've had spot washes all week, have ingrained grime to be scrubbed off necks, ears, elbows, knees, feet, and if we yelled in protest, the soapy cloth found its way into our mouths.

Mrs Wishy-Washy has been a very popular character for nearly thirty years, thanks to Liz Fuller's lovely art.

When we wrote Story Box, we made dummy books and I did rough illustrations so that the books could be tested in schools. Those drawings really were rough, although they were the best I could do, and I later thought it unfortunate that photocopies went to the illustrators who tended to copy my characters rather than create their own. But in the case of Mrs Wishy-Washy, the make-over was very successful. My thinner, grumpy character blossomed into Liz Fuller's large motherly woman who exuded both bossiness and kindness.

Liz is a fine artist as well as an illustrator and I fear that her painting may have been neglected in the years she worked on early reading books. But what a gift she has been to children! Her characters never fail to light up the eyes of a young reader, and I often saw little ones hugging the Huggles books Liz illustrated for Wendy's new programme, Sunshine.

I once visited a private school in Colorado, a beautiful old mansion where children in neat uniforms – unusual for America – sat at polished cherry-wood tables under crystal chandeliers, only about nine or ten to a class.

These children were beautiful in appearance and manners, and they listened politely to my introduction of the big book of Mrs Wishy-Washy. I showed them the front-cover illustration of Mrs Wishy-Washy with a scrubbing brush in one hand and a bar of soap in the other. 'What does this picture tell us about the story?' I asked.

A young gentleman put up his hand. 'Please, Ma'am, she is a domestic.'

In the mid 1980s there was a series of unfortunate events that ended with Wendy leaving New Zealand News. Her staff went with her. So did I, as did most of the Story Box illustrators. Within the next week, Wendy set up her own publishing company, Sunshine Books, and her husband Don helped her to move into a house in Otahuhu.

Wendy's new office had been occupied by tenants with careless cats. No amount of cleaning could lift the sharp aroma from the carpet. We had our inaugural meeting before the furniture arrived and sat on this carpet, drinking champagne and planning the future.

June Melser had retired and was no longer with us. Soon Wendy would increase her staff with Brian Cutting as editor. But at the beginning of the Sunshine Reading Programme, it was just the four of us, Wendy, Bruce, Sandy and I with the ghosts of cats and a bright new challenge in front of us. We knew Wendy. Her positive energy could carve through difficulty like the blade of a bulldozer, and she was always 100 per cent loyal to her own. This was going to work.

Sunshine expanded rapidly attracting a wide variety of authors and illustrators, and overseas markets. The words Wendy Pye were like some international brand name and wherever we travelled, she was mentioned in the context of early reading books.

Having written more than three hundred titles for Wendy, I felt that I was running out of ideas. I wanted to write for children beyond the disciplines required for early reading. Besides, children could not own educational books. They were sold only to schools. So I moved into trade books – titles that were sold in shops and available in libraries: thirty-two-page picture books, chapter books, novels and collections of short stories.

The 1990s were active years. Terry and I had many guests in the retreat house in the bay. There was ongoing writing, school visits to do research and test stories, plus overseas travel to talk at reading conferences and conduct writing workshops.

I still wrote some early reading material, and was invited to Brunei, Malaysia, Hong Kong, Singapore, South Africa, Iceland and Native American reservations, to write stories for their schools. I did a few books but believed that the children of these countries needed their own authors. As a child, I thought there was something inferior about being a New Zealander because I never saw my own country in the books I read. As an author experienced in writing for beginner readers, I could write for my own culture but could not presume to write authentically for others. I decided it would be better if I conducted writing workshops for teachers, encouraged them to record their stories and then helped with the editing and publication. These workshops were largely successful and resulted in children getting their own books.

In the 1990s I also ran writing workshops in New Zealand for people whose culture was not adequately represented in their children's reading. Some of the stories were published for children, and some were printed as collections for local libraries.

During this time Wendy Pye and I kept in touch and I looked on her as a sister. Terry and I visited her family in Western Australia, and we regard Wendy's sister Ellen also as a good friend. Twice we stayed with their mother Marie Jackson, who farmed beef cattle at Cookernup. When I say farmed, I mean that Marie was the farmer, putting up fences, feeding out hay and sleeping in her truck overnight to change the irrigation. She was in her eighties, a marvellous artistic woman with quick intelligence and a tongue to match. She had a great love of the Australian landscape, although with her round-the-clock farm work, we wondered when she had time to paint her landscapes.

It was easy to see the origins of Wendy's dynamic genes . . .

In the late 1990s, I was booked to talk at an International Reading Association conference in Chicago. The Wright Group, the American publishers of the Sunshine and Story Box programmes, asked me to take part in a competition – well, not so much a competition as a draw. Schools around the United States would say why they wanted to have me for a day, and one letter would be drawn as the winner.

All I knew was that on a free conference day, I would be flown to a destination, somewhere between California and New England, Alaska and New Mexico. As it turned out, the winning draw went to a school in Las Vegas, which was not too far from the conference.

I was at the Chicago airport early in the morning with my air ticket and a bag of books for the children. When I checked in, I saw that I had forgotten my passport. Security was strict, but I did have some books with my name and photo on them, and the staff let me through.

That did not work for the flight back to Chicago. The security guards at Las Vegas wouldn't let me go. I still had some books with me, but that seemed only to increase their suspicions. 'Anyone can get a book published with a name and photo on it,' a man said. He then directed me to a small room and said I was to wait to be questioned by a female staff member.

By then, I was concerned that I would miss my plane back to Chicago. I had to give a talk in the morning. What if I could not get on another flight?

It seemed that I was in that room forever. Eventually the door opened and the female security officer came in. My heart sank. She was a strong, stern-looking woman, maybe Hawaiian, maybe Mexican, thin eyebrows, thin mouth and eyes, and I knew from her manner that she was used to dealing with difficult customers. She bustled into the room, slammed the door behind her and looked at me. Then her eyes opened wide and she screamed, 'Joy!'

She was not Hawaiian. She came from American Samoa and had been to a writing workshop I'd done in Auckland.

She enveloped me in hugs and laughter and took me out to the other officers who also became warmly human. I signed the rest of the books for their children before they called a motorised cart to take me to the gate for my flight.

If I were to write of such a happening in a novel, a reader would not believe it; yet how often is life punctuated with events that either defy explanation or stretch it to the limits?

Children's Books
in New Zealand

In the 1990s a group of American teachers questioned me about a worldwide survey done on the recreational interests of young adults eighteen years of age. I didn't know about this survey but apparently, New Zealand eighteen-year-olds had listed reading amongst their top ten pastimes. The teachers thought this could not be true. 'No eighteen-year-old reads books!' one teacher exclaimed.

I said the survey results were probably correct, and didn't apply only to students. I have an example from recent experience, of sitting in a line of traffic waiting for a roadworks operation to be completed. In front of us, a young worker on a bulldozer took a rolled-up paperback out of his hip pocket, flattened it against the steering wheel, and read while waiting for the truck up front to be filled.

A teacher shook her head in disbelief. 'Over here,' she said, 'he would be working on the roads because he couldn't read.'

It's not until we travel overseas that we become aware of New Zealand as a nation of readers. Here, even the smallest town has its library, its bookshop, its school where children are not merely taught to read, they are taught to love reading. Our education system makes full use of children's delight in story, their natural curiosity, sense of wonder, creativity and their expanding interest in language. It caters for the different ways children learn, and is child-centred rather than teacher-directed. There is early emphasis on reading and its overflow into creative writing and art.

This country's literary tradition and its effect of education in the widest sense, no doubt played a significant part in the findings of a college professor in Grand Rapids, Michigan. He told me he wanted to visit New Zealand to see what made us achievers. He claimed that he had researched personal excellence in the world. Take the top ten names in any field, he said, medicine, music, sport, you name it, and one of those names will be that of a New Zealander.

For those of us who find it difficult to believe, a quick personal survey tends to confirm the professor's results; but we may be left with his question: How can this be in such a small population?

How indeed? The small population is a contributing factor. Large, dense populations, of necessity, breed conformity. A small population allows the development of rugged individualism and a pioneer spirit. The rest of the credit surely lies with our education system and a book-loving society.

But New Zealand children haven't always had their own literature. Before the 1950s, very few children's books had been produced in New Zealand, and in schools, young pupils were expected to identify with unfamiliar territory in books from England and America. The New Zealand *School Journals* published by the Education Department's School Publications were the only regular publications in which children could visit familiar landscapes; but because the *Journals* were magazines, many children passively believed that their country was not worthy of real books. This lack was not helped by the popular view that writing for children was a second-rate occupation.

A few publications trickled out in the 1950s and '60s, but it wasn't until the 1980s that we produced a body of children's books that truly celebrated Aotearoa New Zealand. Many of the writers and illustrators had been contributors to the *School Journals*. Jack Lasenby, William Taylor, Bob Kerr, Robyn Belton, Margaret Mahy were some of those who had been nurtured by School Publications, now Learning Media. In the early 1980s Learning Media produced new early reading texts of picture book quality, and commercial publishers, inspired by the international success of Margaret Mahy's books, paid serious attention to the children's market. It was all happening. We saw the emergence of fine Maori writers – Witi Ihimaera, Patricia Grace, Katerina Mataira, Hirini Melbourne. Juvenile fiction was given review space. It found funding with the Queen Elizabeth II Arts Council. It gained its own scholarships and awards.

The New Zealand Library Association's Esther Glen Award for children's books had been with us since 1945 but in 1980 there was established a major national award sponsored by the New Zealand Government. This award put children's writers on a footing with writers of adult fiction, and it created much-needed support for children's writers and their publishers. Over the years, the sponsorship of the award has changed several times, and the award has grown from a simple ceremony that acknowledged excellence in children's literature, to a week-long party that now grips the country from one end to the other. Under the current sponsorship of New Zealand Post, the annual celebration of children's books is possibly the closest thing we have to a true national festival. The countdown starts at the beginning of February when the shortlist for the various categories is announced: senior fiction, junior fiction, non-fiction and picture books. Schools begin their book-related activities: author studies, book character parades, class voting for the best book. Schools also vote for the Children's Choice award that is presented by the sponsor, chosen solely on children's preference. The week before the awards presentation, the New Zealand Book Council has authors and illustrators touring schools. There are storytelling sessions in libraries, children's theatre, literature quizzes, shop windows decorated with posters and book characters, and school writing competitions. Children have designed postage stamps as a part of the celebration.

The actual New Zealand Post Book Awards ceremony is a grand affair, usually held at Government House or Parliament Buildings, but even there, adults share the occasion with young people who have made classroom assessments of the shortlisted books.

This focus on children delights the child in every adult, and it gives authors and illustrators a sense of pride that goes far beyond themselves. Writing for children – once considered the lot of those who had failed at 'real' writing – is now a big international industry, but the real success lies with the enthusiasm of the nation's young.

We know that we can teach children to read, and to hate reading if the learning process is meaningless. Adults don't read dull and difficult material by choice. Why should we expect that of children? We also know from electronic scanning that the human brain learns most efficiently in the emotional context of pleasure. Pleasurable learning leads to pleasurable recall.

It follows, then, that when adults bring children to a love of reading through good entertaining books, books that enchant, nurture and expand young minds, reading will remain a lifetime passion. That passion will create new generations of writers and illustrators, and it will shape the future of New Zealand and its place in the world.

The current government is planning to standardise testing in schools, and teachers are feeling the chill of caution. Standardised testing is the bane of American teachers, who say that it pigeonholes six-year-old children for failure. Yet I can understand a need for some kind of conformity in the United States, a big country where each state has its own school system. In New Zealand, a small country with all schools under the umbrella of the Ministry of Education, I wonder why standardised testing is to be introduced.

Here, all young students are monitored by their teachers – a system that has the advantages of testing without the disadvantages. The children who fall behind on numeracy and literacy scores are usually those whose culture and learning needs cannot be adequately met in big classes. If the money that is to be poured into more paperwork, more bureaucracy, was spent reducing class size – no more than fifteen pupils in a class in the first three years – we would notice a big difference. There should also be free breakfasts in low decile schools.

Can we afford to do this? There is a saying: 'If you think education is expensive, try ignorance.'

There is plenty of evidence these days, to show there are children who are not physically coordinated for reading until they are seven. Some are even older. I have a friend, a school dropout, who became a mathematician at fifty, and he likes to joke, 'I didn't know I had a brain until I was thirty.'

I know that if standardised testing had been around in my day, I would probably have been marked for failure; likewise my son Edward and many other late bloomers I have known.

So where has the parliamentary push for standardised testing come from? I suspect it is somehow attached to the myth that New Zealand once had the highest reading scores in the world.

This is not true.

Reading tests were done with fourth-form high school students fourteen years of age. People of my generation remember them well: mini-exam papers that appeared without warning. The questions were easy enough but there were so many that we rarely finished them all. It was only years later that we discovered what they were for.

Of course we did well enough, because we were readers. The children who could not read were not tested because they had been retained in primary school, fourteen years old, illiterate, in standard five or six, some even held back in standard three, waiting for their fifteenth birthday so that they could leave school.

Many of my generation remember these big children in our primary school rooms. I sat in classes where more than 50 per cent were non-functional readers.

If the move for standardised testing had come from New Zealand teachers I would have been very surprised but would have paid serious attention to it. That it comes from people far removed from the classroom gives me great concern.

There are some excellent initiatives that invest in the education of the next generation, the biggest being Storylines, the Children's Literature Foundation of Aotearoa New Zealand. I have the privilege of being a patron of Storylines and a trustee, and I know the impressive amount of voluntary work that goes into the annual Storylines Children's Literature Festivals, and the other celebrations and awards. I also know how difficult it is to raise money for these endeavours, through begging letters, auctions, raffles.

Around the country, the free Storylines Family Day attracts approximately 50,000 people, most of whom could not come if there was a cost. Finding money for this is such hard work. Wouldn't it be wonderful if we could get a regular government grant?

Through more than forty-five years of writing for children, I've been aware that adults control children's literature from the original idea to publication and purchase. I thought that, while classroom research was important, it was also necessary to test manuscripts in schools before sending them to the publisher. A number of teachers helped me do this, but I also did it myself. It was useful to experience first-hand the reaction to a story: where the energy was low; where the audience laughed; what was understood or not understood. Children do not dissemble. Their feedback is direct and valuable.

One day in a Blenheim school, I tested four manuscripts with a year two class. Two stories were okay, one needed work and the fourth, a story that I particularly liked, received little interest. It was one of those 'message' stories that writers can't resist, from time to time.

'What's wrong with that story?' I asked.

The boy in front of me did not hesitate. 'It's boring,' he said.

I decided that I could rewrite it or, at least, recycle parts of it in another story; but I needed more specific information. 'Which bit was boring?' I asked my young critic.

'All of it,' he replied.

He was right. The story went into the trash pile.

More than once, I've mentioned the valuable relationship that develops between an author and an editor. Over the years, my editors have also become good friends. Anne McCormick, my first editor, has been a close friend for more than forty years and although she has not been my editor for most of that time, we still share lives and will continue to do so. I have worked in easy and rewarding companionship with Bernice Beachman of Penguin New Zealand, Patti Gauch of Philomel, NY, Penny Scown of Scholastic and Frances Bacon of Clean

Slate. Occasionally, I've crossed to the other side and done editing for publishers in Australia and the United States, and have greatly enjoyed occasional editing work in the Auckland Scholastic office. This gave me contact with a number of writers, and in the early days it brought the realisation that while writers of books for adults had local networks and support, New Zealand children's writers felt they were on their own. I contacted friends Tessa Duder and Gaelyn Gordon with the idea that we should have a children's writers and illustrators hui in Fish Bay at Easter 1993.

Like all things meant to be, it happened, and the weather – often bleak at Easter – smiled on the plan. Twenty-five writers and illustrators came to Fish Bay by car, water taxi and float plane, and thus began four days of laughter, music, discussions fortified by Easter eggs and lubricated with wine, and initiatives that were to have considerable consequence for children and children's books.

The merry company included Sherryl Jordan, Joanna Orwin, Robyn Belton, Pauline Cartwright, Ged Maybury, Diana Noonan, Margaret Beames, Ruth Corrin, Tessa Duder, Trevor Pye, Martin Baynton, Joan de Hamel, Jean Bennett, Elsie Locke, Gaelyn Gordon, Diana and Gary Hebley, William Taylor, Philip Temple, Dorothy Butler, Christine Ross, John Bonallack, Jennifer Beck, Paula Boock and Mona Williams.

Everyone had been told to arrive with two offerings: a current question or concern and an item for a concert. Most of the contributions for the evening concert came from authors reading their own works, many very funny; however, no soliloquy could compete with the play staged in a small space around the dining table, by Tessa Duder, Martin Baynton, Gaelyn Gordon and William Taylor – a performance that left us all weak with laughter.

Accommodation space was crowded with comfort on the edge of school camp standard, but somehow that added to the feeling of camaraderie. The sky was clear blue, the sea as green as the trees, and the bay wrapped its arms around us as each shared with the group the lonely space of a writer or illustrator. Most of the questions concerned publishers and marketing. Mine was about neither, a question so far out on a wishlist that I couldn't see it happening: Wouldn't it be wonderful if writers and illustrators could put on a free festival day for children?

The idea could have died there and then, except that Tessa and Gaelyn picked it up and ran with it. The following year, the three of us worked to organise a free family day at the Auckland Museum, which had kindly donated a venue. Staff at the Museum said they usually got about a thousand visitors on a Sunday: they expected that number would double with the extras. The family day was well advertised, sponsors helped with balloons and printed materials, and the Children's Literature Foundation lent their support. Can you imagine what the Museum staff felt half an hour before starting time, when they looked out and saw their vast sloping lawn packed with families? An estimated ten thousand adults and children were waiting for the doors to open.

Although the Museum was overcrowded, there was no damage, merely a lot of excited noise as children ran from one storytelling session to another or helped illustrators at their craft. At the end of the day, we could not believe how successful it had been. We were all tired, but not so exhausted that we couldn't start planning the next year's celebration.

The Children's Literature Foundation took over the organisation of the festival, the name Storylines was coined and it became an annual event, growing in size and scope every year. Which just goes to show that an idea can be a powerful engine, but only if someone puts wheels under it.

New Zealand children's writers and illustrators are now also well organised, and since that Fish Bay hui, there have been several larger gatherings and workshops that have consolidated communication and support. Some writers have joined the American-based Society of Children's Book Writers and Illustrators (SCBWI), which now has an Australia/New Zealand branch, and the New Zealand Society of Authors has become a welcoming body. Generally, within our country there is new awareness of writing for children as something better than 'the occupation of those who have failed at real writing'. The standard of published children's literature here is very high, and it attracts the attention of overseas publishers. Many of our illustrators also work for publishers in other countries: David Elliot, Robyn Belton, Elizabeth Fuller, Gavin Bishop.

If you took four million people out of any big city in the Western world, how many of them would be professional writers and illustrators? The answer is a guess – not many. Then comes the next question: Why does New Zealand produce so many good children's books? That answer is simply: I don't know.

Chautauqua

In 1990 Wendy Pye introduced me to Kent Brown and the Highlights Foundation and from that evolved many wonderful years on the faculty of the Highlights Writing Workshops at Chautauqua, New York.

The Chautauqua Institution is a walled village on the shores of Lake Chautauqua about an hour from Buffalo, and for three months of every summer it becomes a holiday camp for the arts. Time bows backwards in this place: the wooden houses, dwarfed by old trees, have white wicker chairs on their porches and vases of gladioli waiting in anticipation of a visit from Scott Fitzgerald. During the day, people listen to lectures, squirrels flow through leafy shade, and children play at the fountain. Here, Terry and I have listened to talks by Deepak Chopra, Joan Chittister, Sir Edmund Hillary, Barbara Brown Taylor, Al Gore, and at nights we have listened to concerts in the amphitheatre while little back bats obligingly swooped on insects that hovered over the orchestra.

In this rich mixture of music, art, drama, religion, politics, healing, the Highlights Foundation plant an intense week-long workshop for people who want to write for children. By intense, I mean that the faculty/student ratio is one to four and the days are organised to give maximum learning experience in a positive environment.

Going back every July meant that a part of me stayed there, anchored by love for Highlights, the Brown family, the other faculty members – especially good friends Kent Brown, Patti Gauch and Peter Jacobi, plus the many writers who still keep in touch – and, of course, the physical environment. Terry and I developed the habit of going to Chautauqua a week before the Highlights workshops and, in a room on the top floor of the Maple Inn, I would open the laptop on the table by the window and pour out a children's book that had been in my head all year. Writing was easy there. Maybe the energy came from the squirrels that crossed the branched paths of the trees outside, or maybe the influence came from the Carey Inn opposite, and the window that was an eye to the room where George Gershwin composed *Rhapsody in Blue*. Whatever, inspiration was as high there as it is in Fish Bay. At Chautauqua I have written *Snake and Lizard*, *Ticket to the Sky Dance*, *Hunter*, *The Wishing of Biddy Malone* and *Chicken Feathers*. I've also had the pleasure of seeing other New Zealand writers at the Highlights workshops: Margaret Mahy, William Taylor and Frances Plumpton on the faculty; Jillian Sullivan as a confrère.

Because Terry can no longer travel long distances, I've missed four years at Chautauqua, but I will be going back in 2011 to reconnect with the place and those people who have become close family. When I wrote to Kent Brown and his wife Jody to tell them that I could come back, Kent replied: 'Jody's cat was surprised to see me do cartwheels since I have not done that before.'

I think that describes well the special friendship we all share.

English Second Language

Working with children in many countries has reinforced an understanding that the world of childhood is the same everywhere. Children have a keen sense of justice, dislike strong-flavoured food and love jokes. In harsh environments, overcrowded slums and refugee camps, children laugh a lot more than do the privileged adults of the West. That they appear solemn and perhaps a little frightened in media images says more about the moment with the alien photographer than the children's own sense of well-being.

Because most schools have English as a first or second language, I have been blessed by the laughter of children in many countries. I have been hugged by many small arms and taught much about the learning needs of children in their early years at school.

I've had interesting moments outside the classroom – on a grumpy runaway camel in Egypt; in a sandstorm in Jordan; in a Borneo head-hunter's house with a basket of human skulls hanging outside; gathering berries on the tundra in Alaska; sleeping with children and a young goat in a fourth-class railway carriage in India; joining

South African children in a soccer game with an empty Coke can as a ball; being dive-bombed by nesting terns in Iceland; crash-landing in a hot-air balloon in Kenya; and drinking yak-butter tea in Ladakh. These moments appear like snapshots in memory; but the greater images come from the teaching I've had from children.

At a school in Amman, Jordan, I learned a lesson about 'talking down' to children. Usually, when I'm working with a class of new entrants, I like to give them an opportunity to ask questions, but I'm aware that many do not understand the difference between a question and a statement, so I usually offer an explanation. To these children, I said, 'You know what a question is. You ask it when you want to find out something. For example, I could ask you, "Why do trees lose their leaves in autumn?"'

A five-year-old boy put up his hand and said, 'It's because the chlorophyll level drops.'

The teacher put her hand over her mouth to hide her laughter. I'm sure she's still telling that story to her friends.

Visitors to Hawaiian schools are often given lei of sweet-scented flowers. One morning in a school in Oahu, I received a lei from every class so that by lunchtime my shoulders had disappeared in a fragrant garden. As I left the last class, a six-year-old boy stopped me at the door. 'I have another lei for you,' he said, holding up something that looked like a black cord. I glanced down at his feet. Sure enough, one of his shoelaces was missing.

I leaned over and he carefully draped the shoelace around my neck. Twenty-four years later, I still have it. It sits in a box of small treasures and I take it out from time to time and hold it. You can't put a price on gifts from the heart.

It was late summer in Barrow and the local men were riding their quad bikes, wearing T-shirts and shorts, while I was wrapped in layers of wool topped with a heavy coat, a thick scarf across nose and mouth to prevent air cutting like a razor blade. The Arctic desert was still covered in snow. I couldn't tell where the land ended and the Arctic Ocean began.

The teachers at the local school put trays of water on a window ledge for five minutes to get ice cubes. Oil heated the inside of the buildings and my morning with the children was spent in hothouse temperatures.

The Yupik children were reading books in two languages – English and their own. Because books will not be printed in the language of smaller nations, the publishers and I agree that teachers should do their own translations and paste their language over the English text.

Most of the children had conversational English and we talked a lot that morning about polar bears. The teachers expressed alarm at the number of children's picture books depicting polar bears as cute, fluffy and benign. These bears do not hibernate, they said, and people mean only one thing to them: food. A full-grown bear can easily knock down the door to a house.

The children told me in a matter-of-fact way of people they knew who had been killed by bears, and of bears that had been killed by local people. Children were not allowed to play outside – they had their own playground inside the school. Adults did not go ice fishing on their own. Barrow had a bear patrol, a wagon that cruised around the village on the lookout for danger.

At the end of the morning, one of the teachers told me that a whale had been brought in and was being cut up on the beach. Did I want to see it? Yes, I did. We wrapped up in warm clothing, got in her 4WD vehicle and drove past the houses to a snow-bound beach where three men were at work with chainsaws and ulu – which are traditional round-bladed knives.

Because no vegetation can be grown on the Northern Slopes, the people depend on whale meat as it constitutes a complete diet. They take whales with care. Two will keep a village for a year.

Although this whale had been brought in the day before, it was frozen solid, and red ice flew from the chainsaws like sawdust. The teacher and I took photos of the men, and they then gave us their ulus to take pictures of us.

After that, we drove back to the school for an afternoon session on closed-circuit television, in which I talked to children in other schools on the Northern Slopes.

Another teacher told us that she, too, would like to see the whale, so after school we got in the 4WD and headed back along the track.

From a distance we could see that the whale was stripped down almost to its bones and the men were no longer there. But something else made our driver put her foot on the brake. A polar bear on its hind legs was raking strings of flesh from the ribcage, with long sharp claws. The bear was not white as I'd supposed, but a creamy yellow colour. It was very big.

The vehicle went into reverse and we quietly backed away, our driver telling us that a bear of that size could easily turn a vehicle over and rip it open.

When I visited schools in the townships near Johannesburg, I learned that the publicity given to Soweto had earned it international aid. Other townships had not received the same attention and were very poor. They did have schools, and that was better than the blackboard under an acacia tree I saw in a small South African village, but these township schools were overcrowded. I wondered why all the pupils had pencils so short they could barely grip them. Then I discovered that a classroom teacher cut her allotment of thirty pencils in half or even thirds so that each pupil could write. Their paper was pieces of newsprint torn off a roll.

Yet the shining faces crammed into a room were full of positive intelligence. Many of these children spoke several languages – Xhosa, Swahili, Zulu, Afrikaans, English, as well as a smattering of European languages for the benefit of tourists who bought at souvenir marketplaces. I was struck by two things: how happy these children were, and how mature. At eight and nine years, they were not concerned with childish things, and instead of asking about my country, children and favourite book, the important question was, 'How can I get a good job?'

I fervently wished that I had an answer.

On a Tohono O'odham reservation in Arizona near the Mexican border, I worked in the school at Indian Springs. The children were gentle, close to each other, and if I asked one a question, he or she would not immediately answer but would confer with others and then give back a consensus reply.

One morning I arrived early in a classroom empty except for three small boys who sat together on a rug. The child in the middle sat still and silent, his face utterly passive and running with tears. The boys on each side of him were also expressionless but they had their arms around his shoulders and were holding him close.

I asked a stupid question of the crying boy: 'Is something wrong?'

He didn't reply, but after a few seconds one of the others said, 'This morning an eagle took his puppy.'

In Unalakleet, a native village in the Alaskan Bering Strait area, some teachers and students put on an afternoon tea for me, with their traditional foods. The teachers, who had come from southern states in America, warned me that I'd be given blueberry ice cream. 'It's not like our ice cream,' they said. 'It's made of whipped reindeer tallow, seal oil and blueberries. The people here know that we don't eat it so they won't be offended when you refuse.'

Refuse? I was determined to try it.

The beginning of the meal was delicious – dried salt salmon and some kind of chopped deer meat plus cubes of fermented whale meat that looked like black and grey liquorice allsorts. The whale, caught in spring, was cut up and the meat put down with salt and herbs, against the permafrost. After a while it became mildly alcoholic. It tasted quite fizzy and, I have to admit it, delicious.

Then it was time for the bowl of blueberry ice cream. True, it didn't look like ice cream. I took a spoonful and with a show of confidence put it in my mouth. My Western taste buds were not prepared for the grease and strong fishy taste. When I swallowed I had to fight to keep it down and, at the same time, maintain the interested smile. Everyone was watching. I held my breath and took another spoonful. Oh, it was awful! Worse than the castor oil our mother gave us when we were constipated. It brought back vivid memories of being held down on the floor, my nose pinched so that I'd have to open my mouth for the oil spoon.

But I did eventually finish the bowl. The teachers and children were impressed. I was the first outsider to eat it! They wanted to give me a second helping.

This time, I had to refuse.

The next morning, my body told me what it thought of blueberry ice cream. Yes, it definitely was worse than castor oil.

Above Barrow, Alaska. Pretending to cut flesh from a whale.

Below Japanese preschoolers rolling in 'mud' as pigs in the story of
  Mrs Wishy-Washy.

Above In Waitaria Bay School.

Right Terry's boat, *Mrs Wishy-Washy*, moored in Fish Bay.

Above 1998, Judith, Sharon and me.

Below The whanau Cowley. Back row: John Vickers, James Cowley, Sharon Cowley Vickers, Judith Cowley, me, Terry, Weston Cowley, Maria Cowley. Front Row: Charlotte Vickers, Tim Vickers, Loren, Richard Vickers, Oscar Glossop, Lucy Vickers, Edward Cowley, Janice Cowley (five grandchildren absent).

Above The Sounds. With grandsons Oscar and Edwin, circa 1993.

Below 2008, eight grandchildren. From front left, clockwise: Tim, Richard, Lucy, Max, Oscar, Weston, Edwin, Charlotte.

Left Bungy jump for my sixty-fifth birthday, 2001.

Above Writing under the watchful eye of my 'editor'.

Below Portrait of me by Glenda Randerson in her series of New Zealand writers.

Above Terry and I, 2010.

Karunai Illam

In 1984 I went to India with friend and author Jean Watson. Jean is a Vedantist, and since India was her spiritual home, I believed it was important that she go there. At the same time, Malcolm had been invited to the vineyard of a friend in Tuscany, to be part of the *vendimia*. Malc planned to leave a few days after us, and it was agreed that I would meet him in London.

With Indrail passes, Jean and I travelled around the north of India, with particular interest in holy sites. We went as far north as Kashmir and Ladakh, and returned to Delhi for a few days' rest before the rest of the trip. Jean wanted to see Benares. I wanted to go to Bede Griffiths ashram in the south. But while we were planning the route, Jean phoned her son Harry in New Zealand. Harry told her that I needed to get in touch with my family, urgently.

Malcolm had not left for Italy. He had become seriously ill with lymphoma and was in Wellington Hospital.

I flew back to New Zealand. Jean travelled on by herself. Somewhere in the Dindegul province she met Subbiah, a poor weaver, and his wife Mariammol who were looking after some orphaned children and could barely afford to feed them.

That was how Jean's successful orphanage, Karunai Illam – House of Grace – began in Nilakottai.

Over the last twenty-five years, the Illam has nurtured and educated hundreds of orphans and children from destitute families. Five years ago, Terry and I visited the Illam with my grandson Max, to open a new building. We met many people who had been raised in the Illam and had come back to pay their respects – tradesmen, nurses, teachers, computer technologists. I looked at these strong, confident adults, and the happy children who would one day be in their shoes, and I glimpsed a pattern of threads in the tapestry of connection.

If Malcolm had not become ill, Jean and I would have continued our planned tour of holy sites in India. Her orphanage, and all that has flowed from it, would not have happened.

Grandchildren

In December 1982 when our beautiful Lily was born, I crowed new status like a rooster on a rooftop. An older neighbour congratulated me on the first grandchild. 'Welcome to the SOGPIPS,' she said.

'Sogpips?'

She chuckled knowingly. 'Silly Old Granny, Photo in Purse.'

I knew what she meant. Nothing prepares us for the utter delight that comes with the next generation of babies. We become a little unhinged from serious responsibility and do wild things with grandchildren like staying up late, bouncing on the furniture, looking only at the restaurant dessert menu, and allowing them to wear their gumboots in the house. If parents complain, we can always tell the grandchildren what Mum or Dad was like when they were young.

Since Lily, another twelve have been gifted to us. Sharon and John have four: Lucy, Richard, Charlotte and Tim. When Edward married Janice he acquired three teenage stepsons: James, Oliver and Ben. Judith and Greg had three boys, Oscar, Max and Edwin, and a daughter

Phoebe who died soon after birth. James and Maria have Weston, and we also include Maria's son by a previous marriage, Jason. This lot, with the extras we claim as family, make a goodly tribe, and when we are together in the Sounds, we feel like a small village.

When the grandchildren were young, they did not connect Granny with Joy Cowley. That came late, causing some of them embarrassment, while others made capital of it.

I was having a phone conversation with six-year-old Edwin, against a background of noise from his playmates, voices ricocheting off the walls. Edwin, who had always called me Granny, turned away from the phone. I heard him yell, 'Be quiet! I'm talking to Joy Cowley.'

I didn't know whether to laugh or wince.

Gaelyn Gordon told me about a visit to Northcote Primary School. She was trying to tell stories to new entrants but a cherub with white curls and a fierce blue stare kept interrupting.

'I've got a snail in my pocket,' the cherub announced.

'That's nice, dear,' said Gaelyn and went on with the story.

'I got it in the garden.'

'Did you, dear? Well, when we've finished you can put it back in the garden. Now let's listen to the story.'

'I can't put it back,' said the cherub. 'It's squashed.'

Gaelyn went on reading.

But the child was not going to be ignored. She fixed Gaelyn with a blue stare and said, 'Joy Cowley is my grandmother.'

Gaelyn told me that at this point she put her hands on her hips and said, 'I might have known!'

With the arrival of great-grandchildren, we've had the pleasure of seeing a second and now a third generation of family embraced by the bay.

When the grandchildren were preschoolers we'd go out with a small bucket on a treasure hunt, gathering moss, green pine cones, bits of white quartz, a seashell or two, a feather, the koru of a fern, gumnuts and karaka berries, sometimes the shell of a dead crab or weta. There was always more treasure than our bucket would hold. Then we'd take it back, empty it on the table and tell stories about it.

As they got older, it was fishing, boating and bush walks on fine days, the building of swings and tree huts, attempts at water skiing. Wet weather brought them in to make fudge or bake pizzas, and then there were the crafts – glass-painting, clay models and beads, and drawn thread embroidery with wool on hessian.

Invariably they outgrew Granny's craft sessions. Weston, the youngest grandchild, decided at ten that his place was with his dad, fixing things in the old house. I missed him. However, on the day James had to fly out on a film job, there was a knock on my door. There was Weston looking politely grown-up. 'Granny, I thought you might be lonely and need some company,' he said.

We were back to making clay beads.

Edward and Janice's three boys are serious about motor sports, and a few years ago the oldest, also called James, took me boy-racing with his friends. They didn't go on roads but on tracks through scrub near a river, and on this raining day, the track was as greasy as a larded pig. What a marvellous ride! I was in awe of the way these boys handled their vehicles. We slipped and slid, skidded, stalled, did donuts and figure eights until the cars were covered in mud.

I hadn't had such an adrenalin rush since the days of loops and barrel rolls in a Tiger Moth.

I wish it could be possible for boy racers to have their own off-road events centre.

In our family we believe it is better to give each other experiences than 'stuff'. For many of the grandchildren, experience has been associated with Terry's 37 ft Pelin launch called *Mrs Wishy-Washy*, a beamy boat that was outfitted like a floating caravan. For a week or two every summer we flew a pirate flag and had the pirates aboard – grandsons Oscar, Max and Edwin, who were all keen seafarers. We would spend most of our time around D'Urville Island, fishing and exploring during the day, reading the latest Harry Potter aloud in the evening. If the weather and tides were favourable, we'd poke our noses out into the deep holes past Stephens Island and catch groper. Oscar got seasick in heavy swells but as soon as we started catching fish, he'd be off his bunk and out on deck.

Twice on those summer trips, the boys helped us to rescue boats in distress – one a runabout in French Pass, the other a fishing boat that had filled with water in a storm. They became adept at boat handling, tying nautical knots, fish filleting and snorkelling for paua. One day they will pass these skills on to their children and grandchildren.

Other Kinds of Wisdom

Old fishermen told us that before a southerly, cod swallowed stones as ballast and went to the bottom to ride out the weather. I thought it sounded like a bar-room tale until we went out fishing in the gap between a southerly and a nor'wester. Sure enough, each cod stomach was full of gravel. Humans can't always predict when a southerly will arrive. How do fish know? Change of barometric pressure? But how is that registered 80 metres below the surface?

When I'm filleting fish, a crowd of gulls fly behind the boat, screaming, dipping this way and that, but they never collide; neither do the autumn starlings that whirl like tea leaves in the sky, or the school of herring that wheel and turn as one. With a cool weather change, masses of white jellyfish fill the bay, congregating so close in parts that, from a distance, the bluish rings on their surface look like a purple oil slick. Yet two hours later there is not a jellyfish to be seen.

The more I observe animals, the more I believe they have some kind of collective intelligence of which we, in our egocentric states, are completely ignorant.

I am reminded of Mark Twain's comment: 'Man is the highest creation. Now, I wonder who found that out?'

In 1969 I received an odd letter from the United States. Someone called Cyril Clemens said that the Mark Twain Society had made me an adopted daughter of Mark Twain. I put it aside as some kind of hoax. I'd had a few begging letters and was certain that this would be followed by a request for money.

One night after work in the pharmacy, I went to a restaurant, had a solitary meal with a glass of red wine, and went back to a silent house. I was in no mood for writing but I saw the odd letter on my desk and wound paper into the typewriter: *Dear Mr Clemens. It is an honour to be the adopted daughter of Mark Twain but if I had been born at a different time, in a different country, I would have preferred to be his mistress.*

I put a stamp on it, walked down to the postbox, and then forgot it.

A few months later, a large envelope arrived from America. The Mark Twain Society was authentic, well respected, and there was my letter plastered over a front page of its magazine.

Today I wouldn't be concerned. I've made a fool of myself so many times, that now I accept clangers as normal; but this was 1969, and for weeks I whimpered with embarrassment.

When we were allowed to set nets in the bay in summer, we sometimes caught eagle rays, commonly called stingrays. These are beautiful creatures and they do not 'attack' people, although they will whip their tails and raise their barbs in defence if someone treads on them or, more foolishly, tries to ride them like surfboards. Fortunately their gills are so placed that they do not die in nets and Terry and I were always able to release them. We'd bring the net into shallow water and gently unwrap them, touching, talking, letting them know that we intended to set them free. We believe they knew that. They didn't struggle but watched us with their deep-set doggy eyes. Of course, we avoided touching the barb. Once I had impaled my hand on a ray barb and was filled with the worst pain I've ever experienced. Still, we had to get close to the barb and tail to untangle the net, and the rays allowed us to do that. When the net was clear, we'd gently touch their wings to steer them into deeper water. Then we'd watch them swim away, as graceful as ballet dancers.

It doesn't surprise me to hear marine biologists say that rays are as intelligent as dolphins.

Terry and I were on the boat, fishing for groper in deep water past Stephens Island. We'd caught nothing, the tide was about to change and it was time to pack up. But then I got a massive bite which I suspected was a groper – though when you are fishing at 600 metres it's hard to tell. Whatever it was, it was big. About halfway up, the fish was still active and I knew it was probably a shark. It took me a long time to get it to the surface.

Yes, it was a shark but not one I'd seen before. It was beautiful, the shape of a thresher, big bullet-shaped body and long tail, but a light brown colour with darker brown spots. The poor thing was exhausted and so was I. As it opened its mouth, I saw that the hook was caught in a fold of skin near the back of its throat. 'I think I can release it,' I told Terry.

I gave Terry my rod to hold, and grabbed the bait knife. Then I leaned over the side of the boat, put my hand in its mouth and nicked the skin. The hook fell out and the big shark sank under the surface.

Only then did I realise how stupid I'd been. If that shark had closed its mouth on my hand and dived, I would be dead. Terry and I were talking about that when there was a splash near the boat. It was the same shark. It broached like a whale, leapt high out of the water, turned and went back in. When it came up it made eye contact with us.

We stood there in silence. There was nothing to say. That's the problem with mystery. As soon as you try to define it you dishonour it.

The birds in the bay react to humans in different ways. The weka are so bold that they will bring out their chicks at an early age, balls of dark fluff, and will peck our feet if we are late with our offering of whole grain bread – no white bread, thank you – and fish scraps. Tui and bellbirds come close; likewise the paradise ducks, oystercatchers and shags. But the grey herons will shriek in alarm when they see us, and fly away, voicing disapproval.

The kingfishers also scold. There were several perching on a manuka branch above the goldfish pond. They were well fed and content. However, when we put wire netting over the surface, they squawked for days. We were glad we couldn't understand what they were saying.

One year we brought some American relatives to New Zealand. My aunt had been a war bride and neither she nor her husband had seen the country since the 1940s. They particularly enjoyed their time in the Sounds and we promised that, when we could, we'd bring them back for another visit.

A few weeks after their departure, we were sitting by the fire at night with Parehauraki Huirama, a good friend who visited us often.

It was about 9.00 pm and there was a fantail fluttering at the window. I had never before seen a fantail at a window at night. I knew that Parehauraki believed fantails brought bad news and eventually I had to say to her, 'Look at the window. I think there's a messenger for you.'

She moved to see the bird flapping against the glass, then she turned back to me. 'No dear, it's for you. You saw it.'

The belief that fantails brought news of death was not part of my culture, but I respected Parehauraki's wisdom, and that night my children all got phone calls from me. Everything was fine with them. Why was I phoning so late? No, there was no news.

The next morning there came a phone call from the United States. The previous day my aunt's husband had died suddenly from a heart attack.

I would not insist that the two incidents were connected. All I know is that the more I observe animals the more I suspect that human intellect operates on only one level of reality which is so concerned with control of knowledge that it doesn't allow for other ways of knowing.

I think Mark Twain had a point.

The Religious Gene

A few years ago I was asked to do a talk at the Auckland Writers & Readers Festival, the subject being the influences that made a writer. Towards the end of the talk, I told the audience of about five hundred that I was coming to the greatest influence in my life – spiritual guidance – but I had left it until last because I respected other views. 'I know that some people feel uncomfortable with talk of spirituality and religion,' I said, 'so I won't be at all offended if you want to leave now.'

Two women got up and quietly, graciously, left. I was not prepared for what that would do to the rest of the group, who felt free to talk about religious experience. Indeed, there was such an animated discussion in that room that we went past our allotted time and had to vacate in a hurry for the next speaker.

Now I shall suggest something similar. This chapter is not everyone's cup of tea. If your mind hits a wall when someone mentions religion, skip it or close the book here.

I probably have a religious gene, if there is such a thing. At any rate,

I had a religious upbringing and although I rejected most of that, the rejection was in the form of leaving shallow waters to journey into the deep. It would be true to say that spiritual awareness has always been a part of my life.

Freud called religion the product of a lazy mind. I would argue with that, because if we take any system of rational thought and pursue it, it ends up as philosophy and will then shake off words and become mystery. We cannot know it all, for the spark of the infinite is imprisoned within a very limited sensate system. We may say 'the universe is this, the universe is that', but what we should say is, 'we perceive the universe to be this or we perceive it to be that'. Our little knowledge comes from what we can see, hear, taste, touch, smell. If we had a different sensate system, the universe might appear as a very different reality.

Yet there is a knowing that comes without sensate stimuli, and it sometimes bubbles up, like a clear spring, in deep meditation. Four thousand years ago, Hindu monks described the principles of quantum theory. Today psychics help police solve crimes. For the rest of us, there are always experiences that we can't explain, and we tend to put them aside in the face of our doubting intellect, almost embarrassed because they suggest a range of notes off the regular keyboard. But something in the deepest part of our being tells us that we are directly connected to a great system of existence.

I don't have a scientific name for this web of connection, so being a simple person I use a simple word. I call it God.

Children live close to that other knowing, and an experience that I thought uniquely mine, I now find is common to many. I used to wake up at night with someone calling my name, and, sometimes, there would be music. I couldn't describe the music. I felt that the sweet sounds were not being played, but that everything in the world actually was music. As soon as I was fully awake, it disappeared.

In the 1980s, when I was doing research in schools, I talked with classes about dreams and some of the children told me about people who talked or sang to them and woke them up. Commonly, children were called by name. One girl said, 'You hear it when you are a bit awake and then you really wake up and there isn't anyone there.'

They all agreed that these experiences made them feel happy and while the voices were familiar, they didn't know who they belonged to.

I don't offer explanation for this, only that a number of children have it and in some extraordinary way, it produces a feeling of well-being. When I was young, I certainly didn't talk about it to adults, for fear of being laughed at, and also because I was quite possessive of these experiences. They belonged to a feeling I had that I was never alone.

As a child I may have had strong creative energy but I also needed practical understanding of phenomena, and since there was no ready explanation for the feeling of being companioned by some 'otherness', I made up stories to fill the gap. One was that I was supposed to have been twins and my twin sister died before my birth, but her ghost did what I did and kept me company. I knew that I'd made up this story, but it was better than no explanation at all.

My dear parents had more hardship than they deserved. They had limited resources financially, physically, mentally and this inevitably showed in fear-filled religion. There were bright moments, happy hymns and stories of Jesus – an adult who actually liked children – but all of this was overlaid with images of a punishing God who said, 'Spare the rod and spoil the child'. The fear washed down on us like acid rain, stripping pleasure, stunting growth. I found my way around it, but in my sisters and brother it caused an intense dislike of religion and it was many years before they got over it.

I once wrote a story that began, *When things went wrong in our house, Mum blamed Dad and Dad blamed the Government.* Someone asked me if this was autobiographical. It wasn't. In our house, all error was dumped on the devil.

Our parents talked a lot about the devil. He made us lazy, made us tell lies and prevented us from keeping our bedroom tidy. The devil had to be whipped out of us. Sunday sermons in church reinforced my parents' hatred of the devil and when I was about eight, the harsh judgements caused a reaction. I couldn't bear to see someone so hated. Each night before sleep, I prayed that God would make the devil good. I knew my parents would be very upset if they knew, but I thought if God could make the devil good, that would solve everyone's problems.

Looking back at that, I saw that what I was doing was probably the first step of a long journey towards wholeness.

My mother grew up in an evangelical tradition that believed a child of seven was at the right age to make a commitment to Christ and be 'saved'. When I turned seven, the pressure began. I wanted to please my mother but I couldn't do what she wanted. I had some vague idea of what it meant to 'give your heart to Jesus' but it seemed a very big thing and I didn't want to do it. I don't think I consciously thought of it in terms of commitment. It was a visceral reaction. When it was mentioned I had a feeling of great heaviness, and I shrank like a snail into a shell.

'Is Joy saved yet?' my Swedish grandmother would say.

My mother didn't answer.

I knew what they were thinking. People who weren't saved went to hell. That didn't worry me too much. I knew that when people died they left their bodies behind, so I didn't see how they could get burned. What concerned me was the anxiety I was causing my mother, her mother, and my aunts.

This state of siege went on for two years. I was late coming to reading, but when I was nine I was given an old Bible my parents had found in a second-hand bookshop. They told me I needed to read it right through every year. I did that most years, although I skipped the boring bits. I'd already been told most of the bible stories that get told to children, and I read others that didn't make sense. 'Adam knew Eve.' Well, of course he knew Eve because she was his rib. And what was wrong with lying down with someone? There was much in the Old Testament that was bewildering. But somewhere in that book, I found the Gospel of St John. Of all the Jesus stories, these affected me the most. They sent shivers down my back.

> The wind bloweth where it listeth and thou hearest the sound thereof but knowest not whence it cometh or whither it goeth. So it is of everyone that is born of the Spirit.

At last I had found words that connected with the experiences I could not define, especially the feeling that I was never alone. What if my made-up twin sister was actually Jesus? Or an angel? I didn't know but not knowing didn't matter. I was nine and a half and it was time. I took a broken plate, some newspaper, rose petals, my father's matches, and went into the pine trees at the back of our house. I lit a small fire in the plate and sprinkled the rose petals on it. I made the commitment and there was no heavy feeling. It was right.

When I told my mother, she cried with relief.

We attended a little Presbyterian church with a caring community that wrapped itself around us. They helped my parents when they ran out of money, which was quite often, by leaving gifts of clothing and food on our porch. I liked the people, and loved the church – an old wooden building that smelled of varnish, flowers and brass polish. On my way home from school I'd sometimes go in and sit in the sun-drenched emptiness.

Sundays we went to Sunday school in the morning and a church service at night. At the end of the year, there was a Sunday school party at which we received a book prize. To actually own a book was a triumph. It didn't take me long to work out that if I shopped around, went to the Salvation Army on Sunday afternoons and the Methodists every second Sunday, I could get three parties and three books each year.

During high school years I taught Sunday school, attended bible class and enjoyed bible class social life, square dances, sausage sizzles, and bible class camps where people sometimes asked if I had considered being a Presbyterian deaconess. At one stage the idea appealed but it was dampened by that old heavy feeling. There seemed to be an inner barometer in me, with two settings: yes and no. When something was wrong, I closed down, no matter how right the choice seemed to the intellect.

Experience of Christian religion gave me tastes of sweetness and also frustration. To use another metaphor of pilgrimage, I ran out of road each time I tried a new path. It seemed to me that Jesus' teachings were so much bigger than the traditions that claimed to carry them.

In my twenties and thirties, I studied other religions. It was difficult to find sources. There were very few books on comparative religion available in libraries in the 1960s, but I did find a few volumes on Buddhism. My husband Ted told our local Presbyterian minister that I was reading these.

The man shook his head. 'You'll eventually come back to Christ,' he told me.

'I haven't left,' I replied. 'I'm still Christian.'

'If you were, you wouldn't be reading Buddhist books,' he said. 'I will pray for you.'

That heavy feeling again! I knew it was time I left his church. It was like an overcoat that had become too tight to wear.

After years of searching, the gift came at a time of great desolation. It was May 1968, and I was struggling with loss so overwhelming that I didn't know how to survive it. I was on my own, depressed, not sleeping, and one Sunday afternoon I took fifteen tablets of Soneryl butobarbitone. It was an irrational act. I tipped the tablets into the palm of my hand, put two back in the bottle in case I needed them, and swallowed the rest. I knew that a recorded fatal dose was seven tablets, yet I did not plan to kill myself. All I wanted was to sleep in a deep place away from dreams and pain.

I lay on the bed crying, but was soon overtaken by a sense of peace. There was a feeling of rapid upward movement. As the room dropped away from me in a waterfall of silver light, there was a great rush of joyous recognition. I was travelling fast into a light I'd always known. It was nothing like the sun. Much, much brighter and alive! A white light that was everything! I was filled with its sweet presence.

This was the light I'd come from and it was taking me back. The feeling of bliss was exquisite. I wanted to laugh at the simplicity of it all. I had total knowledge. There was nothing I didn't know. And what was more, I'd had this experience of homecoming many, many times.

My last conscious thought was, 'How could I have forgotten?'

Then I began to fall. I could still see the light in the distance but I seemed to be dropping down a dark well and I couldn't prevent that from happening. I became very distressed, and struggled to get back. I felt pain, heard voices.

I was in the intensive care unit of Palmerston North Hospital and it was Tuesday evening. The experience had seemed to take about twenty seconds. It was, in fact, three days.

The feeling of rejection was so keen that if I had been able to get to the roof of the hospital, I think I would have jumped off; but I was blind, partly paralysed, had the beginnings of pneumonia and pleurisy and was in a cot with metal bars on either side.

That night and the following morning, I drifted in and out of consciousness but seemed to come awake about 11.00 am. What happened then had the sharp detail of reality and was important to me although even now I don't know what to call it. I toss words in the air – dream, hallucination, vision, out-of-body experience – but none of them fit. All I can say is that suddenly there was no pain and I could clearly see the light all around me, not intense now but like fine gold dust in the air. I moved effortlessly out of the bed and drifted out of the ward and down the corridor in my hospital gown. There were people out there. A doctor with short grey hair and black stubble on his chin walked towards me, the end of his stethoscope tucked into the pocket of his white coat. I thought he would walk around me but he didn't. I felt the gold light shiver as he passed through. No one saw me until I got near the entrance of the hospital. Two young women, standing outside the public toilets, had a pushchair with a plump, curly-haired toddler in a hand-knitted pink cardigan. The child stared at me and turned her head as I went past and out the door.

The lawn and garden outside were filled with light. They looked very beautiful, and sitting in the middle of the lawn was a small old schoolhouse. It was typical of many old one-roomed country schools and I didn't question its presence or my need to visit it. One second I was outside, and the next I was in a room furnished with small desks and chairs. What I saw inside that schoolroom distressed me. There were about a dozen people with adult-sized heads and little bodies, dressed like babies in vests and nappies. They were all people I knew and admired, among them Monte Holcroft from the *Listener*, Professor Joan Stevens from Victoria University, writers Irene Adcock and Louis Johnston, and an artist who had illustrated some of my *Listener* stories. They had been turned into children, no higher than my waist, and these were their desks. It was clear that they were being kept prisoners.

I wondered who had done this to them.

When they saw me, they ran towards me and clung, as toddlers do, and it occurred to me that I needed to find the door and let them out. At that thought, a door at the end of the room opened and in walked a tall, cowled figure in black robes with a school bell in his hand. He ignored me and walked to the front of the room, ringing the bell. The door behind him was left ajar.

The little people left me and ran to form a line in front of the man.

'Tell me your question,' he chanted.

I thought he had a bullying manner, and I didn't know why he said *tell* instead of *ask*.

The little person in front of him was deferential. He asked a question that I didn't hear, and in response, the dark figure gave him a paper-wrapped sweet from the sleeve of his robe. The little person was very pleased and went away unwrapping the sweet as though it were a great reward.

The next one came up.

'Tell me your question,' said the man, and the same thing happened.

I got in line behind the others, and when it was my turn, I stood in front of the figure. I was his height but when I looked into his cowl, I could not see a face.

He rang the bell. 'Tell me your question.'

I didn't ask a question. I simply opened my mouth and a huge noise came out, a noise of storms and earthquakes and sliding rocks. It wasn't my voice. It seemed to come through me from somewhere else in the universe.

It had a strange effect on the monk-like figure, who slid down the wall and collapsed at my feet. When I looked at him on the ground, I saw that he was just a fold of robes, cloth with no substance.

I turned to the little people. 'See? He wasn't real. Now you are free to go!' And I pointed to the unlocked door.

But the little people didn't want to go. They were very upset. They wailed and clutched at the black cloth lying on the floor. I tried again to show them they had their freedom but they ignored me and were inconsolable.

I decided that I would leave, anyway, and as I walked towards the door, I saw a baby in a bassinet. I recognised the face as belonging to someone I knew. I didn't like the man, who was very intense and unhappy, but here he was simply a little baby, fast asleep.

I decided I would take him with me. I pulled back the cover and stepped back. There was no body. It was just a head on a satin pillow.

I looked back at the others, still crouched over the empty robes, and was suddenly filled with a deep sadness. I knew I couldn't go. I had to stay with them and look after them.

I went to one of the windows of the schoolroom, looked at the light outside, and wept. Then I discovered that I was crying in the intensive care unit, and staff were adjusting the oxygen tent over my bed.

I was ten days in hospital. The psychiatrist wrote on his report, *No evidence of psychosis, normal reaction to abnormal stress*, and sent me back home to manage my life.

The light didn't disappear entirely. It was as though some residue was left within me, and like others who come back from near-death experience, I was profoundly changed. I felt so different that for a while I wondered if I had actually died and entered some parallel universe. Everything seemed new, there was an inner strength I hadn't had before. All the fears I'd carried had miraculously disappeared.

Later, I worked out why. When you lose a fear of death, what other fear is there?

The dream or vision I had was so powerful that it continued to haunt me. I recounted it to close friends and family and in doing so thought that in that dream, I was probably given a choice of 'going home' to the light or staying. I also guessed that the insubstantial monk represented my dissatisfaction with the kind of religious dogma I'd found empty – small, feel-good rewards handed out instead of answers to life's questions.

Other symbols I have not yet unravelled, but within three years of that dream, two things happened. A new psychiatric unit was built on the lawn where the schoolhouse stood; and the man whose face was on the baby in the cot committed suicide.

Of this I am certain: when my time of final transition comes, I will be like a child running to meet it with arms outstretched.

My search for meaning took on new focus: references to light in the Gospels and in the mystical writings of all religions. I now knew how to interpret the metaphors, from the Sufi understanding, *Love is the fire and I am the wood*, to the Jewish concept of Ein Sof, to Gerard Manley Hopkins' glory of God 'like shining from shook foil'. Light was not a pseudonym for living according to laws of social good. Light was the greater reality. For me, light was Presence, it was inner truth, it was the 'twin sister' of my childhood, it was everything, and it was always there. When I became busy and stressed, a cloud dulled that awareness; but at other times it seemed that things both natural and man-made, trees, houses, traffic, were painted on a gauze curtain that hung over the light, and everything, no matter how meagre, was beautiful.

When I have one of those moments, I am reminded of a story from India of Sri Ramakrishna, who was walking along a road with some disciples when one asked, 'Tell us, what is sacred and what is profane?'

Ramakrishna did not answer. He walked on a little further and stopped beside a lump of dog manure on the pavement. He bent over, put his finger in it and then pressed his finger to his forehead. Then, without a word, he walked on. They had his answer.

In the 1970s there seemed to be nothing written about near-death experiences, but I met two people who told me how their lives had been transformed. They didn't know how to describe it and one man said there were no words invented for it. But for both the experience involved overpowering light, was ecstatic, familiar and there was a feeling of coming home.

Our good friend and neighbour John Robson, who was then Secretary of Justice, talked about a near-drowning incident when he was a young man, and how reluctant he was to come back to the world. John's wife Katharine was present as we talked, but she didn't comment and I guessed from her silence that she was distancing herself from our interpretation of events. Katharine was a scientist, a very kind and sensible woman, but not at all interested in religious experience.

Five years ago, I was working in the States when I received an email from the family. Katharine, then a widow, had cancer and not long to live. She wanted to see me. So I cut short the trip and flew home to a valued friend who had been part of my life for thirty years.

I guessed that she wanted to say goodbye, but there was more to it than that. As her body weakened she was having experiences of 'light' that she could not explain. She wanted to talk about it.

As we sipped wine together, I asked, 'Does the light feel like a benevolent presence?'

Katharine smiled and leaned back against her pillow. 'It is all kindness,' she said.

In the late 1960s, I stopped going to church. I had been taken to a place too wide for the conventions I'd grown up with, and although each church had given value, each was too small. I felt like a high school kid in a new entrants class. That wasn't arrogance. It was my truth. So instead, I read all I could of other religions, sifting wisdom from politics. I also went to lectures and listened to tapes. I enjoyed expressions of truth in Hindu, Buddhist, Baha'i, Muslim and Jewish writings; but felt at a distance from them. At a certain level all religions spoke of the same experiences of love and light, but the symbols they used for the indescribable belonged to other cultures. My culture was Christian and my religious connection was with the teacher Christ Jesus, whom I saw as the great fire of God. The Bible was familiar to me, whereas the references in the texts of other religions required a mental leap. I did find though, rich nourishment in the writings of Christian mystics from as far back as the anonymous fourteenth-century author of *The Cloud of Unknowing* to present-day Karl Rahner.

At the same time, metaphors of light were appearing in lovely dreams of a great translucent sea – and also of snow. The snow dreams were frequent and indicated search. I would be in a familiar place, a suburban garden, a country road, and I would smell snow. It was always the same smell, a delicate sweet fragrance that seemed to fill me. I'd look up and there, some distance away, would be the mountain, glistening white, and I would be overcome with the desire to get to it. I'd scramble over fences, through the scrub on the foothills, but always would wake up before I got there. These dreams were beautiful and frustrating. I wrote about them in a short story called 'Going to the Snow' that was printed in a Penguin collection.

In the mid 1970s I went to some lectures by a Ramakrishna swami who had a face shaped by laughter, always a sign of a good heart. In informal discussion, I quoted some of the books I'd been reading: Ignatius of Loyola, Julian of Norwich, St Francis, Meister Eckhart.

The swami, who had a feminine image of God, smiled at me. 'The Divine Mother is calling you to be a Catholic.' Then he added, 'You are like a hen, scratching here, scratching there. That is not a way to dig a well.'

His words shocked me into silence. I thought my interest in other religions would have his approval. But to be called a shallow, scratching hen? As for becoming a Catholic, no thank you! That was one church I had not explored and I wasn't going there. While I no longer believed all the anti-Catholic rhetoric I'd heard as a child, I was in a space of freedom and I didn't want to give that up for commitment to institutionalised religion. I could admit to myself that the influences that affected me were Catholic, but that didn't mean I had to become one.

Malcolm spoke often of his travels in the South American continent, and in 1977 he said I would gain a lot as a writer from a similar trip. The children were grown and he would pay for me to fly into Chile and then travel overland for two months. It was a magnificent gift and I was ready to go there and then. Malcolm told me to learn a bit of Spanish first. English was not a second language in most South American countries, he said, and I should start the trip at Isla de Pascua.

So there I was on Easter Island with a phrasebook in hand, aware that my stumbling tourist Spanish was far from adequate.

I stayed with a family who were warmly hospitable. On the night of my arrival, Saturday, they took me to a hall where there was a school concert followed by a dance. All the adults were drinking a local brandy, *pisco*, which was harsh, even with liberal amounts of Coca-Cola. I've never had much capacity for alcohol and by 3.00 am I was quite unsteady and possessed of a fierce headache.

We got on the back of the truck, sleeping children wrapped in rugs, young folk, aunts and uncles, my hostess and her husband and unidentified others, for the drive back to the house. My room was small, whitewashed, a bed against one wall and, on the other, a nail to hang clothes. I went straight to bed and was surprised that the rest of the family stayed up, sitting around the table in the kitchen, talking, drinking coffee.

I soon learned why. At 5.30 there was a loud hammering on the door.

'*Senora! La Missa!*'

I groaned. They were going to church and they wanted me to go too. I called back, '*Soy protestante!*'

That made no difference. They kept knocking and calling, '*La Missa! La Missa!*' and by now church bells were clanging, so close that I could feel their vibration in the bed.

I got up, got dressed and one of the women gave me a scarf to wear around my head. When we went out, I saw that the church was almost opposite the house and there were already people inside. What kind of church had a service at six o'clock in the morning, for heaven's sake!

I followed the others and did what they did, dipped my finger in the water and made the sign of the cross, then bobbed with something between a bow and a curtsy at the end of the pew, before sliding in and sitting down. I glanced at the others, then kneeled. And something happened. I was bone-tired and my head ached, but through all that came peace and a recognition that I could not describe. It was here. What I had been searching for was here. I had come home to the larger place.

After Easter Island, I sat in the back of churches in six South American countries, hearing the Mass in rapid Spanish which sounded like music beyond the meaning of words. Some of the churches were a magnificent mixture of affluence and squalor: a solid silver altar and alabaster angels, and cigarette butts flattened on a stone floor that smelled of urine. For me, this represented the great, wonderful, sprawling mess we call the human condition, spiritual beings on human journey, angels coping with animal form in one way or another. I loved the contrast that came together as oneness.

But that kind of greedy love is not the stuff of commitment. I put it aside when I came back to New Zealand and embarked on another writing project. Still, the influences of the Catholic Church kept crowding me, often in coincidental ways that made me angry. For example, in 1980 I was in Madrid, boarding a bus for Toledo. I made a mistake and got on the wrong bus. It was a pilgrimage tour, about forty women with rosary beads, going to Avila and the convent of St Teresa. I felt that I was being tricked; I was irritable with the trickster and annoyed with myself for considering rank superstition.

Whatever, the closing walls were claustrophobic. Early in 1982 Malcolm and I were at a cocktail party put on by Catholic friends. It seemed to me that I had run out of escape room. As the man of the house poured drinks, I called to him, 'How do you become a Catholic?'

It was an effective conversation stopper. Our host looked at me, saw that it wasn't some kind of joke, and took me into his office.

Well, it was all so easy, really, and exactly right. The Ramakrishna swami had made an accurate assessment, and later, I wondered what all the struggle had been about.

Someone once said that the Catholic Church was a wise old grandmother with a lot of rubbish in her backyard. As an outsider I had seen the backyard. On the inside, I came home to the wisdom and the mystery of a love too great to bear a name.

After I became a Catholic, the dreams about journeying to the mountain ceased. But a few months ago there was a new and profound dream about snow. I dreamed I was in Arohanui, one of the houses in the bay, and it was evening. The family were around me. They had music on and were dancing. I wanted to dance outside but they didn't want me to go out in the dark. 'The dark is dangerous,' they said. When I insisted, they tried to hold me back, but I pulled free and went out into a night that was as black as the inside of a cave. I couldn't see where my feet were, but I danced and danced, and large snowflakes began to fall, a few at first, and then more, each one like a white light. Soon there was so much snow around me that I couldn't see the blackness, and I went on dancing.

I found myself back inside the house, being berated by the family for going out in the dark. I said to them, 'Don't you know? The darkness only exists to serve the light.'

I woke up, startled by words. Maybe this dream is the beginning of a new journey.

Going to Seed

I've been down in the orchard picking quinces, golden yellow, round, furry like warm animals in the hand. I am so grateful to the trees in this place that fill preserving and jam jars and bring sun to winter tables. I ask for the same capacity to give.

We are not unlike a fruit tree in its seasons. There is a growing time for taking in nourishment and building strength. Then there is the blossoming, a time of sweetness, wild bees, a richness of fertility. The fruiting time comes from all of this, in the form of work, the weight of production, paradox, preparation for the future. Then comes the last stage and this, I find, is the most fulfilling.

With much pleasure, I am going to seed.

There is time, in age, for us to learn new things, but I need a little extra time to do so. The old prison of the body is breaking down and I put techniques in place to help memory: make lists, check everything twice, allow extra time for practice. Sometimes the body will not be pushed. I started to learn the piano at sixty-one and by the time I got to Grade 6 my fingers refused the speed required by exams. I'd left it too late. But I still play for myself and there is no one to tell me that my Debussy and Chopin are far too slow. Superbly written music tends to hold together at half the speed.

Woodturning has been another pleasure of age. I've always made basic furniture, bookcases and beds that would make any professional joiner shudder and avert his gaze. Like wool, wood is a natural product that rewards with the gift of the sun and rain that formed it, and there is much satisfaction in finding a beautiful bowl in a lump of tree that has grown, like us, from the bounty of the earth.

When we were renovating the original farmhouse in Fish Bay, I needed to advance the basic carpentry skills taught by my father, and I went to woodwork night classes at Onslow College in Johnsonville. When I had finished the night-class assignment – a rimu refectory bench seat – my teacher, John Hoare, suggested that I might like to try the lathe. I did some spindle turning, four coffee-table legs, and promised myself that one day I would have a lathe.

That didn't happen until 2008. My friend Ross Hardie found me a good Teknatool 1000 on Trade Me, and got me started on bowls and boxes. Last year I did the Aoraki Polytech course with Jim Lowe at his Woodturning School, and this year hope to move on with the applied course. I will never become expert but that doesn't matter. As in writing or spinning wool, it is the process that is so rewarding, creating something new from the old, and at the same time learning the secrets of wool and wood and words.

As we get older, the world becomes more beautiful. We might not discover the answers to the great questions of life that we had in our thirties, but the questions themselves have disappeared and there is an acceptance of life that verges on contentment. We do what we can, give what we can, and really don't care too much about what people think of us. If we don't see well without glasses, there is compensation in excellent hindsight as we review a lot of years in Life School. Experience has brought us to a place of wisdom where we judge neither ourselves nor others. We know there is inherent goodness in everything, and we enjoy the present moment more, now that we don't need to make long-term plans for the future.

For Terry and me, sensuality is enhanced with the knowing that comes with age. Two people sit in silence, gently breathing each other's breath, reading each other's thoughts and occasionally reaching out to touch. Fingertips walk the beloved landscape of flesh, every hill and valley so familiar that there is no separation. We belong. Even when we are standing at opposite sides of the room, it can be difficult to know where one ends and the other begins.

Such are our days. The wild bees no longer sing in the blood, but the honey they've left behind is exquisite.

I still write for children, do some retreat work and am involved with Storylines, the Children's Literature Foundation. That is part of ongoing navigation. But I spend more time now enjoying the pull of the tides and listening to the voice of the wind.

If I walk past a mirror and look beyond the reflection, I see an old woman, sloppy, forgetful, still in love with life, paddling a leaky boat on an ever-increasing ocean of light.

It is all exactly as it should be.

Index